SUPER RED BOOK

BOURNEMOUT

CHRISTCHURCH · POOLE
RINGWOOD

CONTENTS

Page Layout & Road Map — 2-3
2½ Miles to 1 Inch

Bournemouth Enlarged Centre — 4-5
7 Inches to 1 Mile

Poole Enlarged Centre — 6
6 Inches to 1 Mile

Street Maps — 7-64
4 Inches to 1 Mile

Index to Streets — 65

Red Books showing the way

Every effort has been made to verify the accuracy of information in this book but the publishers cannot accept responsibility for expense or loss caused by an error or omission.

Information that will be of assistance to the user of the maps will be welcomed.

The representation on these maps of a road, track or path is no evidence of the existence of a right of way.

Street plans prepared and published by ESTATE PUBLICATIONS, Bridewell House, TENTERDEN, KENT. The Publishers acknowledge the co-operation of the local authorities of towns represented in this atlas.

Ordnance Survey. This product includes mapping data licensed from Ordnance Survey® with the permission of the Controller of Her Majesty's Stationery Office.

© Crown Copyright
© Estate Publications 105-15   ISBN 1 84192 385 0
All rights reserved
Licence number 100019031

www.ESTATE-PUBLICATIONS.co.uk

Printed by Ajanta Offset, New Delhi, India.

Map Legend

- Pedestrianized / Restricted Access
- Track
- Built Up Area
- Footpath
- Stream
- River
- Lock — Canal
- Railway / Station
- ● Post Office
- P P+ — Car Park / Park & Ride
- C Public Convenience
- + Place of Worship
- → One-way Street
- i Tourist Information Centre
- ▲8 ▲8 Adjoining Pages
- Area Depicting Enlarged Centre
- Emergency Services
- Industrial Buildings
- Leisure Buildings
- Education Buildings
- Hotels etc.
- Retail Buildings
- General Buildings
- Woodland
- Orchard
- Recreation Ground
- Cemetery

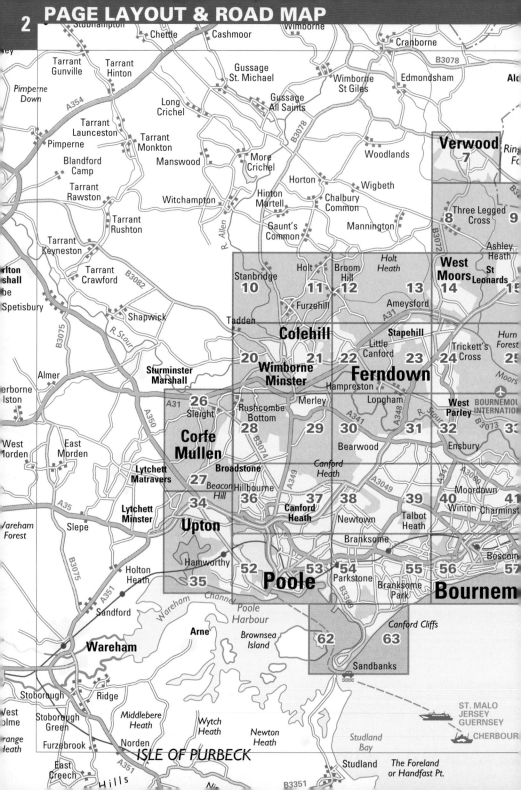

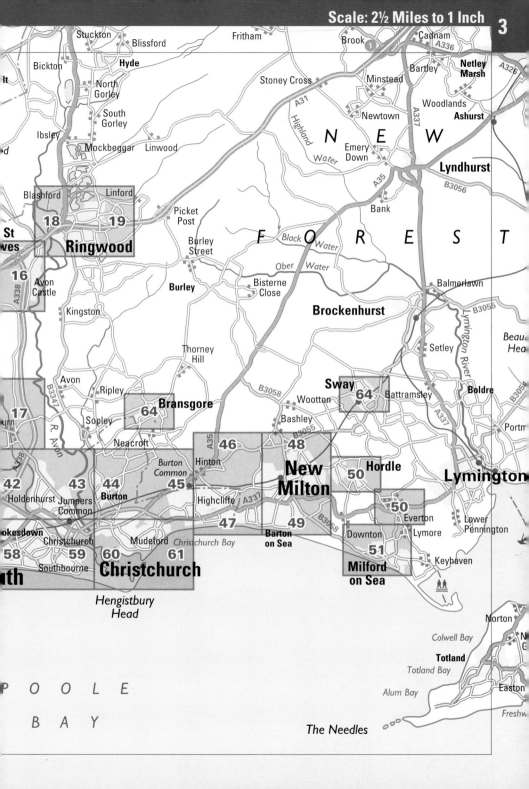

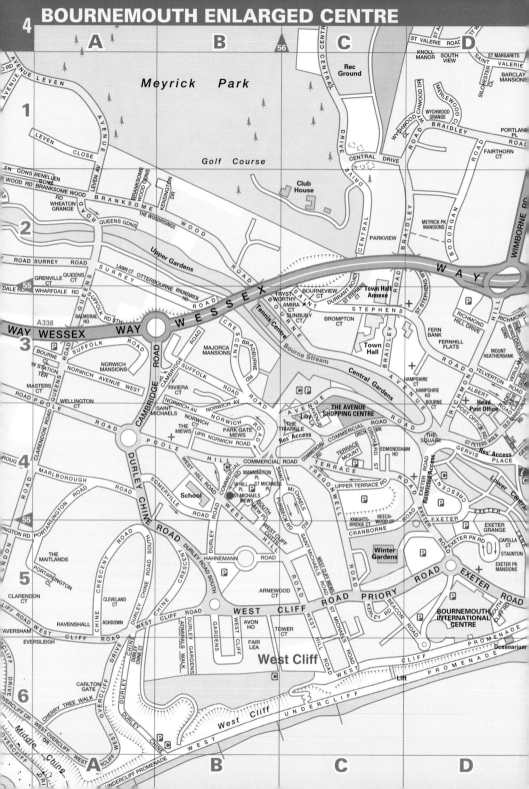

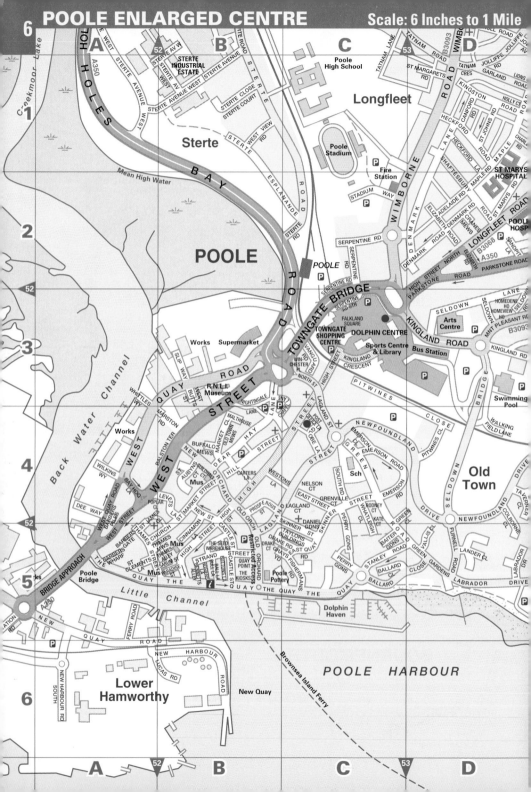

A   B   7   C   D

Potterne Park

omer's Wood

Aqueduct

Potterne Farm

POTTER

B3072 ROAD

work

1

Verwood Manor Farm

Horton Farm

CRAB

Horton Common Crossing

ORCHARD

WAY

Cottage Farm

2

Crab Orchard Farm

VERWOOD

Crab Orchard

Horton   Common

SANDY LANE ROAD

ROAD

Chota Farm

CHURCH ROAD

BROAD MEAD RD

3

School

Lower

DRIVE

ALBANY

CAMELLIA CL

WEST AV

BAY ROAD

FYBES CLOSE

GREEN CLOSE

VERWOOD

Three Legged Cross

Sports Grnd

Caravan Site

Pavilion

N ROAD HORTON

Hall

FRYERS

HERMITAGE CLOSE

BRACKENDALE CT

JOYS

JUNIPER CL

ALL SAINTS

FURZELANDS RD

EARLES ROAD

Rec Grnd

4

GREYCOT CL

RINGWOOD RD

HOLT ROAD

ROAD

ROAD

Homestead Farm

WEST

RINGWOOD

LONGMEADOW IND EST

ROAD

RINGWOOD

SCHOOL LA

LOWER COMMON RD

SANDHURST DR

Homeland Farm

ROAD

FERRY BANK

DYMEWOOD RD

MOORS

HADDONS DRIVE

THREE CROSS COTTAGES

5

Gundry's Farm

OLD BARN FARM ROAD

CRANE WAY

VICTORY CL

Haddons Farm

THORNE WAY

LIBERT CL

Depot

AZURA

WOOLSBRIDGE INDUSTRIAL PARK

6

West Moors Nursery

ROAD

B3072

WEST MOORS ROAD

COLLINGWOOD RD

CONDOR FARM

Sturts

A   B   14   C   D

GUNDRY OR TRADING EST

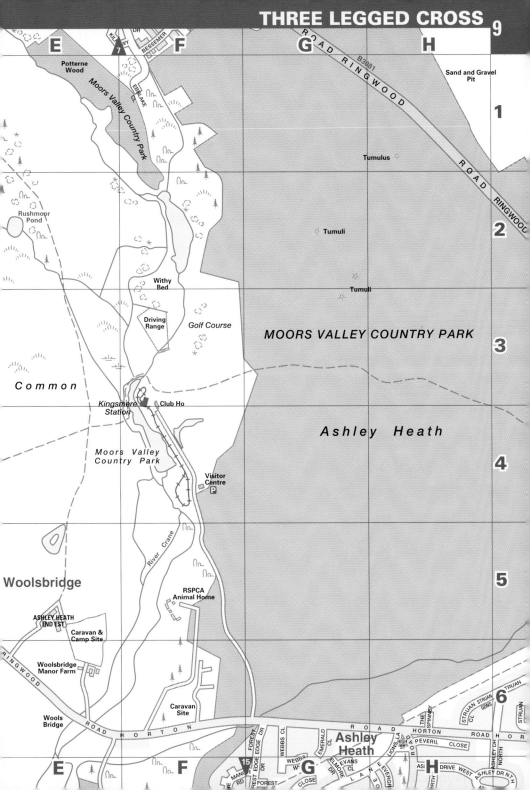

E F G H

Sand and Gravel Pit

Potterne Wood

Moors Valley Country Park

1

B3081 ROAD RINGWOOD

ROAD RINGWOOD

Tumulus

Rushmoor Pond

Tumuli

2

Withy Bed

Tumuli

Driving Range

Golf Course

MOORS VALLEY COUNTRY PARK

3

C o m m o n

Kingsmere Station

Club Ho

Ashley Heath

Moors Valley Country Park

Visitor Centre

4

River Crane

Woolsbridge

RSPCA Animal Home

5

ASHLEY HEATH IND EST

Caravan & Camp Site

Woolsbridge Manor Farm

RINGWOOD ROAD

Caravan Site

6

Wools Bridge

HORTON ROAD

THE SPINNEY

STRUAN

STRUAN CL

STRUAN GDNS

Ashley Heath

ROAD HORTON ROAD HOR

PEVERIL CLOSE

ASHLEY DR NORTH

WEBBS CL

EMERALD CL

ELMORE

EVANS CL

LIONS LA

HIGH ST

MANOR RD

FOREST EDGE DR

FOREST EDGE

WEST FOREST

WEBBS CLOSE

EVERGR

DRIVE WEST

ASHLEY DR NTH

15

E F G H

A   **B** nton Parva   **C**   **D**

Ashton Wood

1

Hinton Mill Farm

B3078

Ashton Farm

Stanbridge

2

Barnsley Farm

Brach Copse

BARNSLEY DROVE

High Hall Copse

3

SPRING HILL COTTAGES

Lower Barnsley Farm

BARNSLEY DROVE

Honeybrook Farm

High Hall

4

Fitches Bridge

GRANGE

The Decoy

5

Higher Honeybrook Farm

Honeybrook Copse

River Allen

Wilksworth Farm

6

Camping & Caravan Site

Pound Farm

A
Hound Hill   **B**   20 **C**   **D**

Catley Copse

BORNE RD

B3078

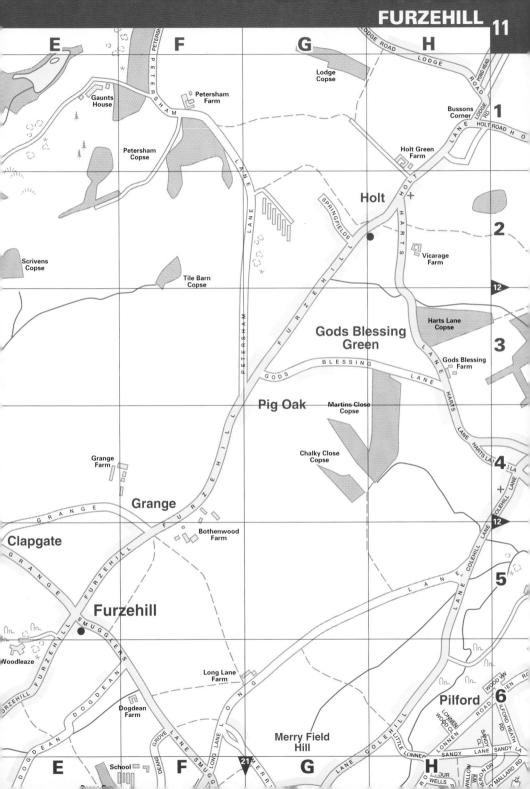

A B C D

1 Broad Bridge · Lussons Corner · POND HEAD · HOLT ROAD · Row Hill · **Higher Row** · Bee Garden Earthwork

2 Drivers Plantation · Pillmoor Farm · P White Sheet Hill

11

3 Lyons Wood · White Moor · s Blessing Farm · *White Sheet*

4 HARTS LA · HARTS LANE · **Broom Hill** · Pilford Copse · *Uddens Park* · Stable Copse · *Park Copse* · COLEHILL LANE

11

5 COLEHILL LANE · Pilford Farm · Daffodil Copse · Garden Copse Farm · White Bridge · Red Bridge · Garden Copse

6 forc · WOOD W · LONNEN ROAD · LONNEN ROAD · PILFORD HEATH RD · SANDY LANE · SANDY LA · Bedborough Plantation · Bedborough Farm · UDDENS DRIVE · UDDE

MALLARD RD · HERON DR · WALLOW W · HEATH

22

A B C D

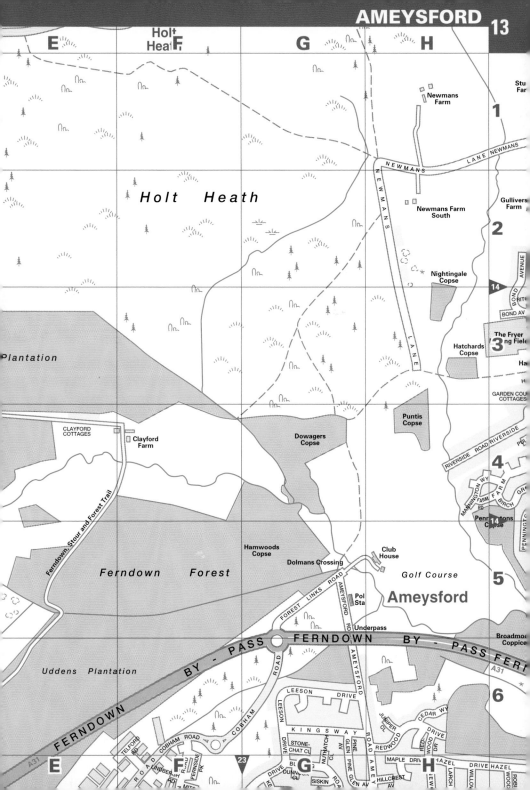

E Holt Heath F G H

1 Newmans Farm — Stu Far

NEWMANS LANE NEWMANS

Newmans Farm South — Gullivers Farm

2

14 BOND AVENUE

Nightingale Copse — BOND AV BRIT

Holt Heath

NEWMANS LANE

3 The Fryer ng Fiel

Hatchards Copse — Ha

GARDEN COU COTTAGES

Plantation

Puntis Copse

RIVERSIDE ROAD RIVERSIDE

CLAYFORD COTTAGES — Clayford Farm

Dowagers Copse

4 MANNINGTON WY FARM RD BIRCH GR

Pennringtons Copse 14

Ferndown, Stour and Forest Trail

PENNING

Hamwoods Copse — Club House

Dolmans Crossing — *Golf Course*

5

Ferndown *Forest*

FOREST LINKS ROAD AMEYSFORD RD — Pol Sta — **Ameysford**

Underpass — Broadmo Coppice

FERNDOWN BY - PASS FERNDOWN BY - PASS FERN A31

Uddens Plantation

6

FERNDOWN A31

COBHAM ROAD — AMEYSFORD RD

LEESON DRIVE

TELFORD RD — FERNSIDE PK — LINDBERGH — COBHAM ROAD — LEESON DRIVE — KINGSWAY — STONE CHAT CL — NUTHATCH — PINE GLEN AV — JUNIPER CL — REDWOOD — CEDAR WY — MAPLE DRIV — HAZEL DRIVE HAZEL — WILLOW — ROO

E F 23 G H

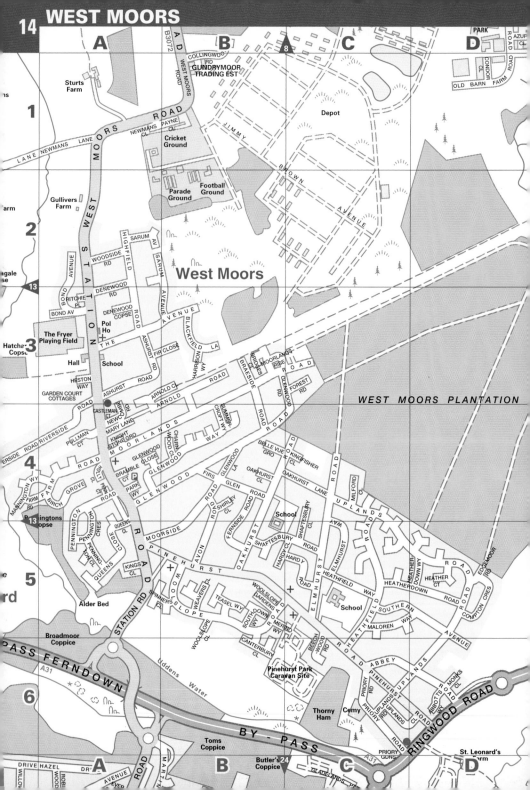

Ashley Heath

St Leonards

Racecourse Heath

Lions Hill

Lions Hill Farm

Little Lions Farm

Moors River

Caravan & Camp Site

Oakhill Farm

Hill Farm

Camping Site

Shamba Farm

Eastmoors Farm

Hotel

ST. LEONARDS HOSPITAL

Camping Site

Leonard's Bridge

Caravan Site

Grange Estate

Hotel

RINGWOOD ROAD

ROAD RING

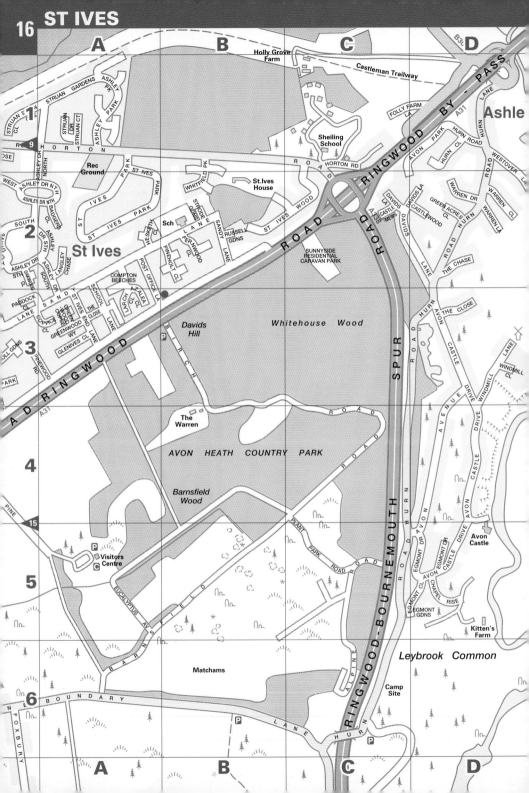

A   B   C   D

Holly Grove Farm
Castleman Trailway
B3

Ashle

1

Struan Gardens
Ashley Pk
Struan Dr
Struan Ct
Ashley Park
Horton
North

Folly Farm La
A31
Ringwood By-Pass
Hurn Lane
Hurn Park
Hurn Road
Westover Road

9
West Ashley Dr Nth
Ashley Dr Nth
Rec Ground
Ashley Dr
Badger
Ashley Park
St Ives Park
Whitfield Pk
St.Ives House
Horton Rd
Ringwood Road
Avon
Davids
Davids La
Warren Dr
Warren La
Green Acres Cl
Castlewood Cl
Warren La

2
South Ashley Dr Sth
Ashley Dr
Langley Chase
St Ives
St Ives Park
Strode Gdns
Sandy Lane
Sch
Russell Gdns
Fernwood Cl
Pineholt
St Ives Wood
Sunnyside Residential Caravan Park
Castle
Davids Mews
Davids Lane
Hurn Road
The Chase

Paddock Lane
Sandy
St Ives Park
Green Close
Greenwood Wy
Glenives Cl
School Lane
The Lane
Larch Cl
Alea Cl
A2
Post Office La
Compton Beeches
Birch
Davids Hill
Whitehouse Wood
Hurn Lane
Avon
The Close

3
Toll Gdns
Pinewood Rd
Coppice Cl
A31
A D Ringwood
P
Road
Road Spur
Castle Drive
Avenue
Windmill Cl
Windmill

4
Pine
The Warren
Avon Heath Country Park
Road
Hurn
Avon
Castle Drive
Egmont Dr
Castle Drive
Egmont Dr

15
Barnsfield Wood
Plant Park Road
Road
Avon Castle
Chapel Rise

5
P
Visitors Centre
Eucalyptus Avs
Barnsfield
Alpine
Egmont Cl
Egmont Gdns
Kitten's Farm

Ringwood-Bournemouth
Leybrook Common

6
Boundary
Foxbury
Matchams
Lane
Hurn
P
Camp Site
P

A   B   C   D

A   **B**   **C**   **D**

Hurn Forest

Fillybrook Bottom

A338

LANE MATCHAMS

Port View
Caravan Park

Mount Pleasant
Camping Park

Avon Common

Furzy
Copse

Bournemouth
Flying Club
P

Pithouse
Farm

Moors River

Lords
Piece

Museum

Pussex
Farm

ROAD

THEOBOLD
RD

BRACKLEY
CL

PUSSEX

South East
Sector

Troublefield
Copse

MOORS
CLOSE

Hotel

AVON

CAUSEWAY

CAUSEWAY   AVON   CAUS

Camping &
Caravan Site

*Sopley
Common*

MCINTYRE

PARLEY

3073

PASSENGER
& CARGO
MAIN ENTRANCE

Hurnbridge
Farm

LANE

MILL

Hurn
Bridge

AVON MATCHANS

CHRISTCHURCH

Sports Club
P

Hurn

Mill Copse

Home
Farm

*Ramsdown
Plantation*

HURN   COURT   LANE

LANE

North
Lodge

Quomp Copse

ROAD

CHRISTC

T   D   us

A338

73

42

A   **B**   **C**   **D**

1   2   3   4   5   6

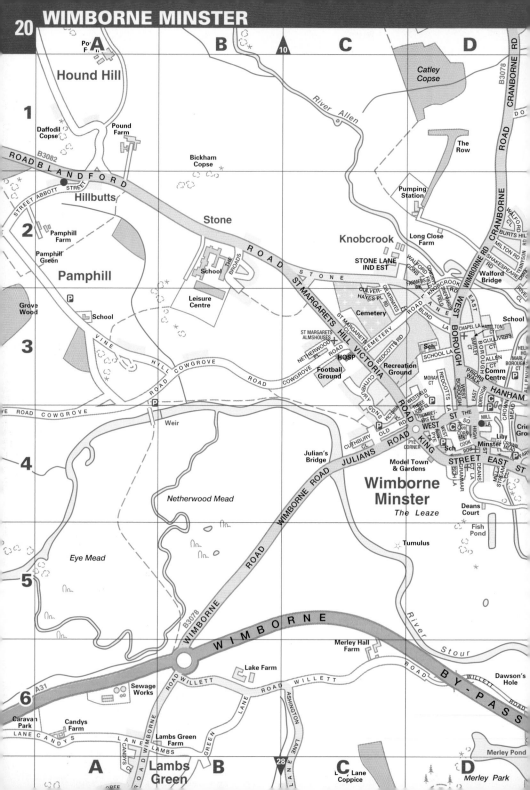

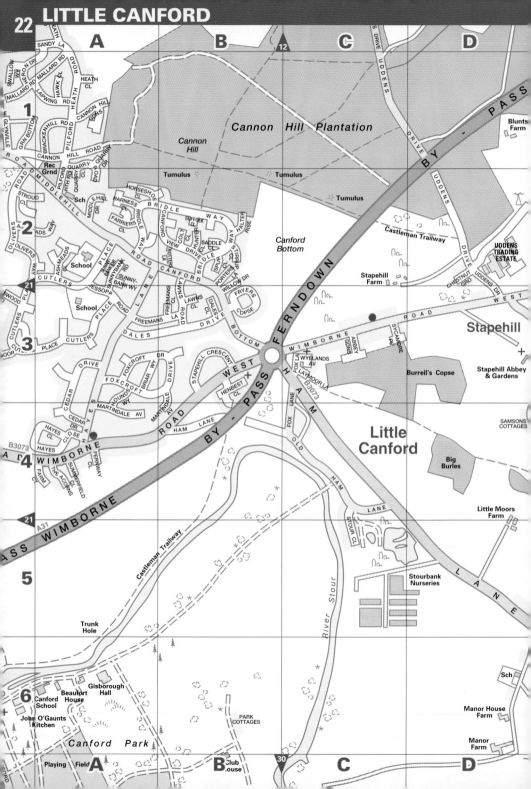

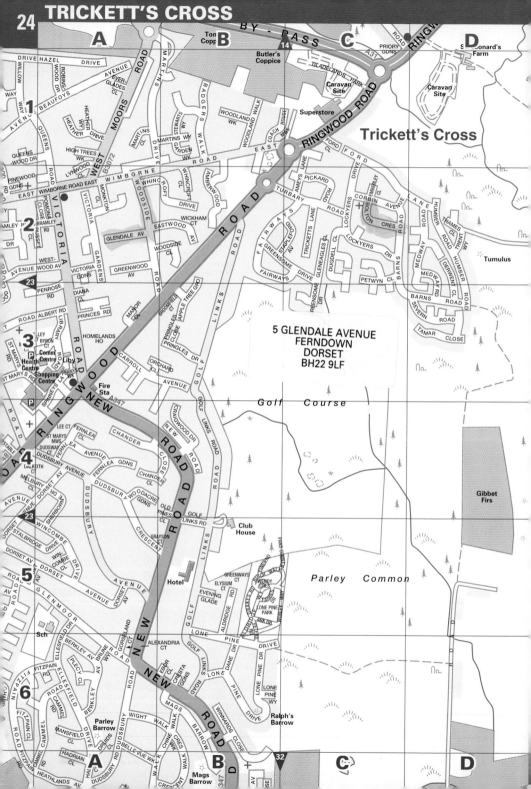

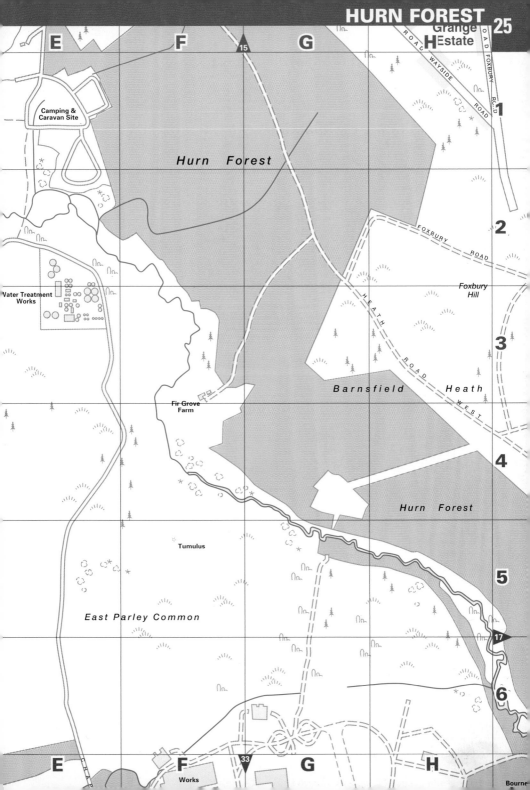

E   **F**   15   **G**   Grange **H** Estate

ROAD WAYSIDE ROAD

FOXBURY ROAD

1

Camping &
Caravan Site

Hurn   Forest

FOXBURY   ROAD

2

*Foxbury
Hill*

Vater Treatment
Works

H E A T H

3

R O A D

Barnsfield   Heath

WEST

Fir Grove
Farm

4

Hurn   Forest

Tumulus

5

East Parley Common

17

6

E   **F**   33   **G**   **H**

Works

Bourne

Corfe Mullen

Hill View

Stony Down Plantation

Poor Common

Cherretts Clump

Beacon Hill

Beacon Heath

Lytchett Heath

Black Hill

Round Hill

Forest Hill

Decoy Pond

Saw Mill

Stony Down Farm

Corfe Mullen Clay Pit

Beacon Hills Clay Pit

Beacon Hills Pits

Brick Works

Beacon Hill Farm

The Holme Bush P.H.

Naked Cross

Nursery

Caravan Site

Dairy

Caravan & Camp Site

Old Sandpit

Lytchett Heath Farm

Pit Bottom Spinney

Jubilee Cross

Resr

BLANDFORD ROAD

NORTH

WAREHAM ROAD

BEACON HILL LANE

A350

A350

HIGHFIELD ROAD

SPRINGDALE ROAD

CORFE LODGE ROAD

WAREHAM ROAD

CHAPEL ROAD

GORSE ROAD

5   6   7   8

F E D C B A

28   36   34   34

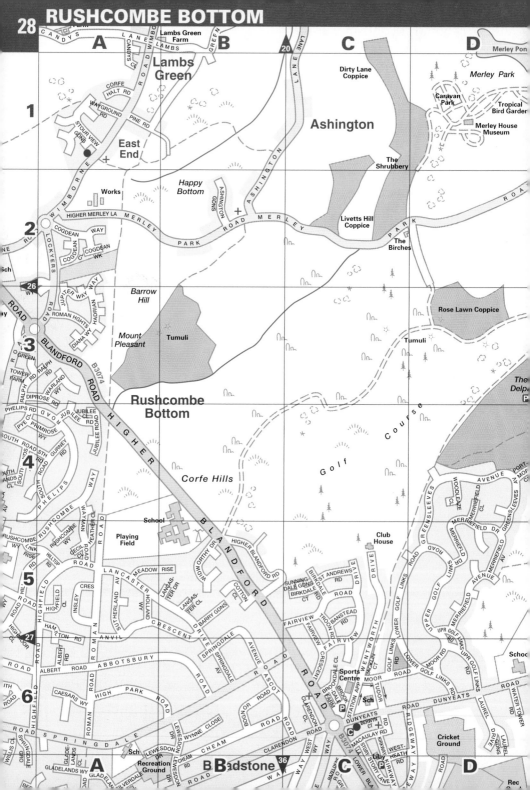

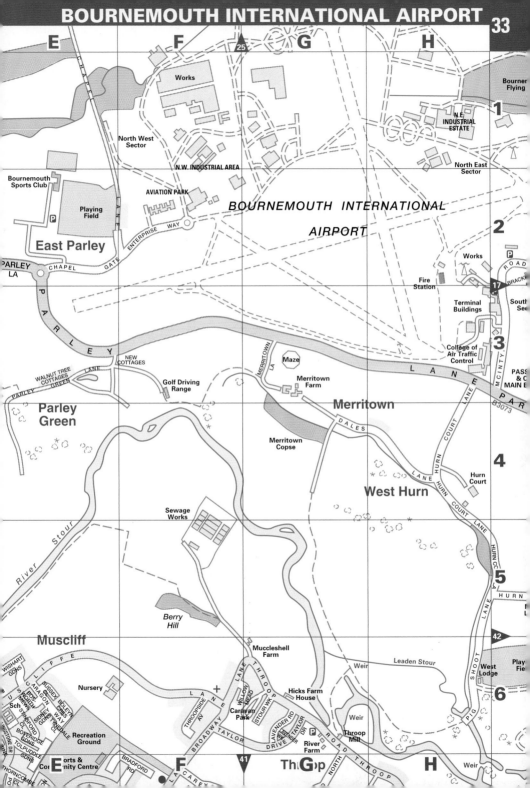

E F G H

1
2
3
4
5
6

Works

North West Sector

N.W. INDUSTRIAL AREA

Bournemouth Sports Club

AVIATION PARK

Playing Field

East Parley

PARLEY LA

CHAPEL

ENTERPRISE WAY

GATE

PARLEY

Bourner Flying

N.E. INDUSTRIAL ESTATE

North East Sector

BOURNEMOUTH INTERNATIONAL
AIRPORT

ROAD

BRACK

Works

Fire Station

Terminal Buildings

South Se

College of Air Traffic Control

MCINTY

17

PASS & C MAIN E

WALNUT TREE COTTAGES GREEN

NEW COTTAGES

Golf Driving Range

Parley Green

Merritown Farm

Maze

MERRITOWN LA

Merritown

DALES

HURN COURT LANE

LANE

PAR

B3073

Merritown Copse

Hurn Court

West Hurn

4

HURN COURT LANE

River Stour

Sewage Works

5

HURN CC

HURN L

Berry Hill

42

Muscliff

WISHART GDNS

Nursery

Muccleshell Farm

WILLOW MEAD

THROOP LANE

STOUR WK

Hicks Farm House

Leaden Stour

Weir

West Lodge

Play Fie

PIG SHOOT LANE

6

Caravan Park

Recreation Ground

orts & Cor nity Centre

BRADFORD RD

LA CAREY

BROADWAY

TAYLOR

THROOPSIDE AV

LANE

LAVENDER RD

LAVENDER DR

TAYLOR DRIVE

River Farm

NORTH

ROAD

THROOP

Throop Mill

Weir

Th G op

41

E F H

LANE

BLANDFORD ROAD

B3068

SYMES RD

S

KEYSWORTH ROAD

GOATHORN CL

RICE GDNS

HEWI

UPWEY CL

WINSPI

RIDGEMEAD

W
6

52

ALMER RD

DAWKINS

CARISBROOKE

FRESHWATER DR

GALLOWAY RD

CARTERS

DAWKINS ROAD

DAWKINS AVENUE

Fire Sta.

HAMWORTHY JUNCTION

MARYLAND RD

LEBERE RD

MID D

MARLIN

Schools

REDHORN CL

SHIPSTAL CL

RUSSELL

FORELAND RD

PEVERELL RD

PATCHINS RD

PATCHINS RD

EGMONT

SOUTH HAVEN CL

Community Centre

Turlin Moor

Sports & Recreation Ground

Schools

GARDENS

FITZWORTH

JUNCTION

ROAD

Hamworthy

Ham Hill

WALCHEREN

ROAD

NAPIER

ROCKLEY PARK Caravan Park

Rockley Sands

Sailing School

Marina

NAPIER

Rockley Viaduct

Holton Point

Rock Lea River

Lytchett Bay

Mean High Wa

Otter Island

East Holton Farm

HERCULES

ROYAL ROAD

NATHAN GDNS

DELILAH

GOLIATH

SAMSON

BENJAMIN RD

JACOBS ROAD

CUMBER

JOSHUA

DAVID WAY

KANGAW PL

NORMANDY

Amphibious Training Unit Royal Marines

ROAD

NAPIER LAKE

Ham Common

Wareham Channel

Rockley Point

Rockley Jetty

NANT

JOEL

ELLI

ROAD

SALERNO

LAKE DRIVE

LULWOR

BRANKSEA AV

LULWORTH

BRANKS

CRES

Lake

MORCONIUM QUAY

Marina

Pontoons

Pier

P C

POOLE HARBOUR

Wood Bar Looe

F

E

D

C

B

A

5 6 7 8

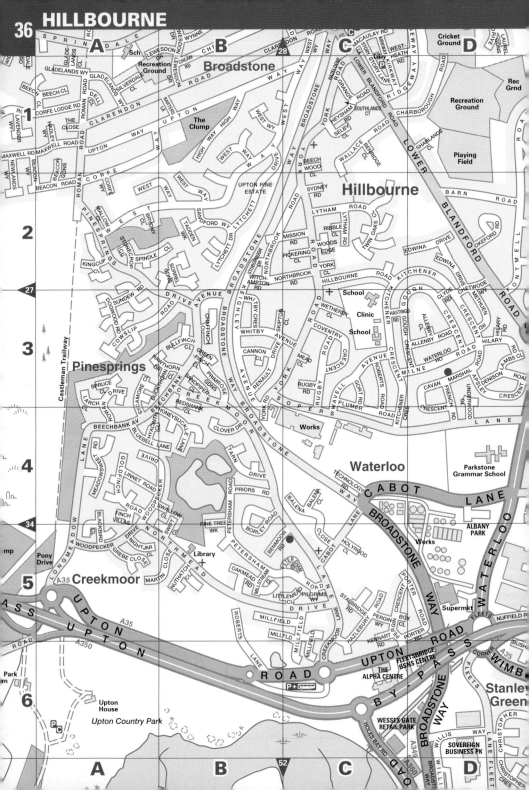

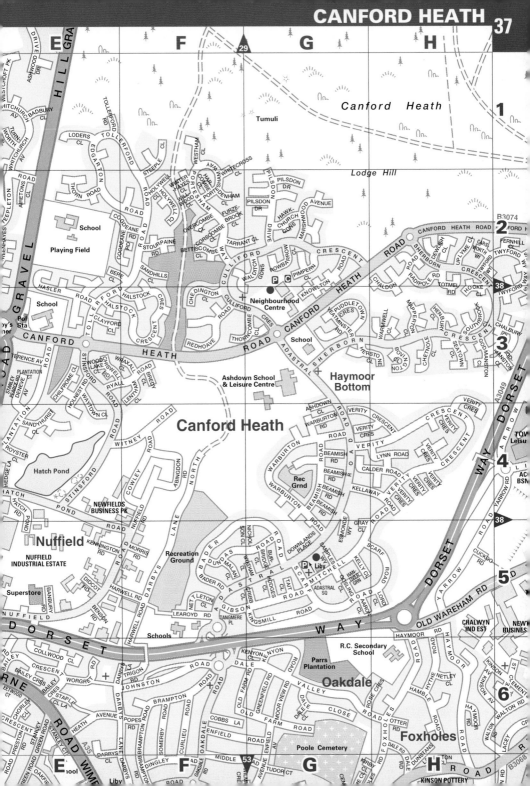

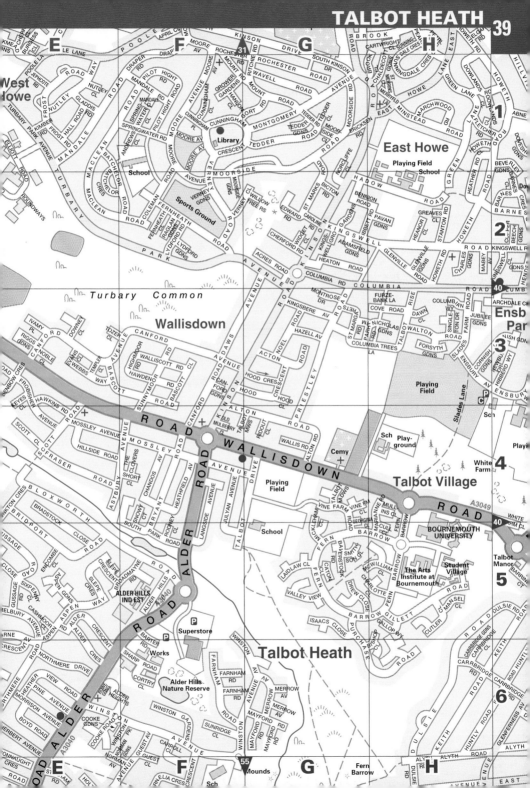

A
B
C
D
1
2
3
4
5
6
Winkton
School
Jopps Corner
WINKTON HO
BURLEY ROAD
BOCKHAMPTON ROAD
SALISBURY ROAD
South Bockhampton
Hawthorn Farm
Hawthorn Farm
LYNDHURST ROAD
Waterditch Farm
WATERDITCH LANE
Avon Valley Path
BURTON CROFT
CAMPBELL RD
CAMPBELL ROAD
CAMPBELL PARK CL
CHESTNUT WY
School
BURTON HALL
BURTON HALL PL
THE LINDENS
PRESTON LANE
HILL LANE
HAWTHORN ROAD
FARWELL CL
KATHERINE CHANCE CL
WINKTON CL
PRIORY VIEW ROAD
AVON RUN
AVON VW
HEATHLANDS
BRINSONS CL
MOORCROFT AV
WOODSTOCK RD
VICARAGE WY
Sch
Burton Green Farm
SUMMERFIELD CL
BARLANDS CL
PITMORE RD
VINNEYS CL
MOORCROFT
BURTON GRN
BURNHAM RD
MEADOW LA
FERN CL
CRABTREE CL
PITMORE RD
PRIORY
COWLEYS RD
BIRCH AV
CLIFFE RD
STONY LANE
B3347
Burton
WHITEHAYES CLOSE
WHITEHAYES RD
WHITEHAYES ROAD
FOOTNERS LA
BODOWEN CL
BODOWEN RD
TREEBYS CL
SALISBURY RD
HOLLY GARDENS
SUMMERS LANE
Playing Field
MARTINS HILL CL
SHORTS CL
HILL LANE
ALDER CL
MEDLAR CL
GORDON WY
MARTINS ROAD
BURTON CL
SANDY PLOT
LINESIDE
Burton Farm
STAPLECROSS LA
Staple Cross
Staple Cross Farm
Sewage Works
AMBURY LANE
WATERY LANE
CHRISTCHURCH BY-PASS
A35
CHEVIOT CT
DORSET ROAD
CHARLES RD
MALLORY CL
Sch
Recreation Ground
IRVINE WY
HILLARY RD
HUNT ROAD
EVEREST ROAD
DRUITT ROAD
EDWARD ROAD
SCOTTS GREEN
SOUTHEY ROAD
Sch
AMETHYST ROAD
COLERIDGE GREEN
School
Playing Field
BONINGTON CL
TENSING RD
REDVERS RD
SLINN ROAD
DRAPER ROAD
SARAH SANDS CL
VICKERY WY
TROAK CL
DRIVE
KNOWLES CL
BATTEN CL
MASTERSON CL
HAKING RD
CHANT CL
MILLER RD
NORMANDY
WOLFE CL
MARABOUT CL
MEREDITH CL
LE PATOURE CL
SMITH CL
BURTON RD
BINGHAM RD
60
SOMERFORD ROAD
B3059
NEWLANDS RD
PENNANT WY
CAXTON CL
WILVERLEY
SEA VIXEN IND EST
SOMERFORD BSNS PK
HUGHES
PUREWELL CROSS RD
PUREWELL
B3059
Arewell
ORCHID
43
43

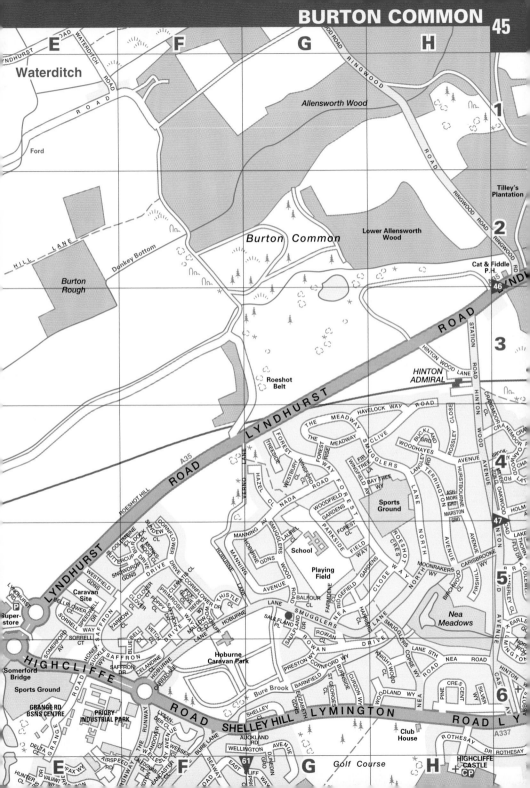

Hordle

A   B   C   D

1

48

2

3

EVERTON

Everton

4

5

6

A   B   C   D

51

Hordle labels:
Rec Ground, Downlands Farm, SILVER STREET, Pennys Corner, Belford Farm, Flanders Farm, EVERTON ROAD, LAUREL CL, ASHLEY LANE, VAGRS LA, STOPPLES LANE, HOLES CL, BLENHEIM CRES, WINDSOR RD, PINEWOOD, STONELEIGH AV, LARCH DR, ELVIN CL, FIRTREE, YERVILLE GDNS, CHARNOCK CL, SYCAMORE RD, ACACIA RD, MYRTLE MONTEREY TIFFANY, WESTMORELAND CT, HAW LA, LAVENDER ROAD, HEATH ROAD, DANECREST RD, CHARLTON CL, DUDLEY AV, STOPPLES LANE, WISBECH WY, Woodlands Caravan Park, Nursery, HEATHER RD, VICARAGE GDNS, SLADE CL, COTTAGERS, WHL BARN CL, MALLARD CL, SHELDRAKE GDNS, COCK LANE, Hollybush Farm, Kings Farm, Arnewood House, Sch, TURNERS FARM CL, FARM CRES, LONGFIELD, BERRYFIELD RD, ELIZABETH CRES, PEGASUS AV, ST MARY GRO, SKY END, SYLVAN CL, Poultry Farm, The Roughs, KINGS FARM LA, EVERTON ROAD, VICARAGE LANE, HORDLE LANE, Danes Stream, Breakhill Copse

Everton labels:
EVERTON ROAD, Icehouse Plantation, WAINSFORD, Rec Ground, GREENMEAD AV, WAINSFORD RD, BUCKSTONE CL, Newlease Copse, Efford House, Knighton Caravan Park, Manor House, FRYS, HONEYSUCKLE GDNS, SHEPHERDS WY, Nurseries, GOLDEN CRESCENT, FOREST WY, EVELEA, CLOSE LANE, HARTS, BEACON CL, FOX FIELD, WEST LA, CENTRE LA, EAST LA, FIRMOUNT, Efford Farm House, ELKHAMS CL, CROSSWAYS, CHRISTCHURCH, YEOVILTON CL, ROBERTS CL, KNIGHTSCREST PARK, FARMERS WK, RODBOURNE CL, OLD CEDAR DR, CHERRY TREE CL, OAK BURNUM WD, WAINSFORD RD, PLANTATION RD, Everton Grange Hotel, THE GRANGE, A337 ROAD CHRISTCHURCH ROAD MILFORD, GRANGE CL, LYMINGTON ROAD, LYMORE LANE, EFFORD HORTICULTURAL RESEARCH STATION, Newlands Manor Farm, BRAXTON COURTYARD, Great Newbridge Copse, BARNES ROAD, Newlands Manor, Fish Pond, Camping & Caravan Site, Cox's Bridge, B3058

Milford on Sea

Lymore

Downton

Pergins Island

Creekmoor Lake

Upton Lake

Holes Bay

Sterte

Manor Park

Sterte INDUSTRIAL ESTATE

STANLEY GRN IND EST

FLEETS ESTATE

SOVE BUSIN D N PK

POOLE

Cobbs Quay

Marina

Back Water Channel

WEST QUAY ROAD

WEST STREET

Works

Supermarket

School

Rec Ground

Liby

Sch

Hamworthy Park

Paddling Pool

School

BLANDFORD RD

Poole Bridge

BRIDGE APPROACH

Works

Marina

Lower Hamworthy

New Quay

Little Channel

NEW QUAY ROAD

NEW HARBOUR ROAD W

NEW HARBOUR ROAD

NEW HARBOUR ROAD SOUTH

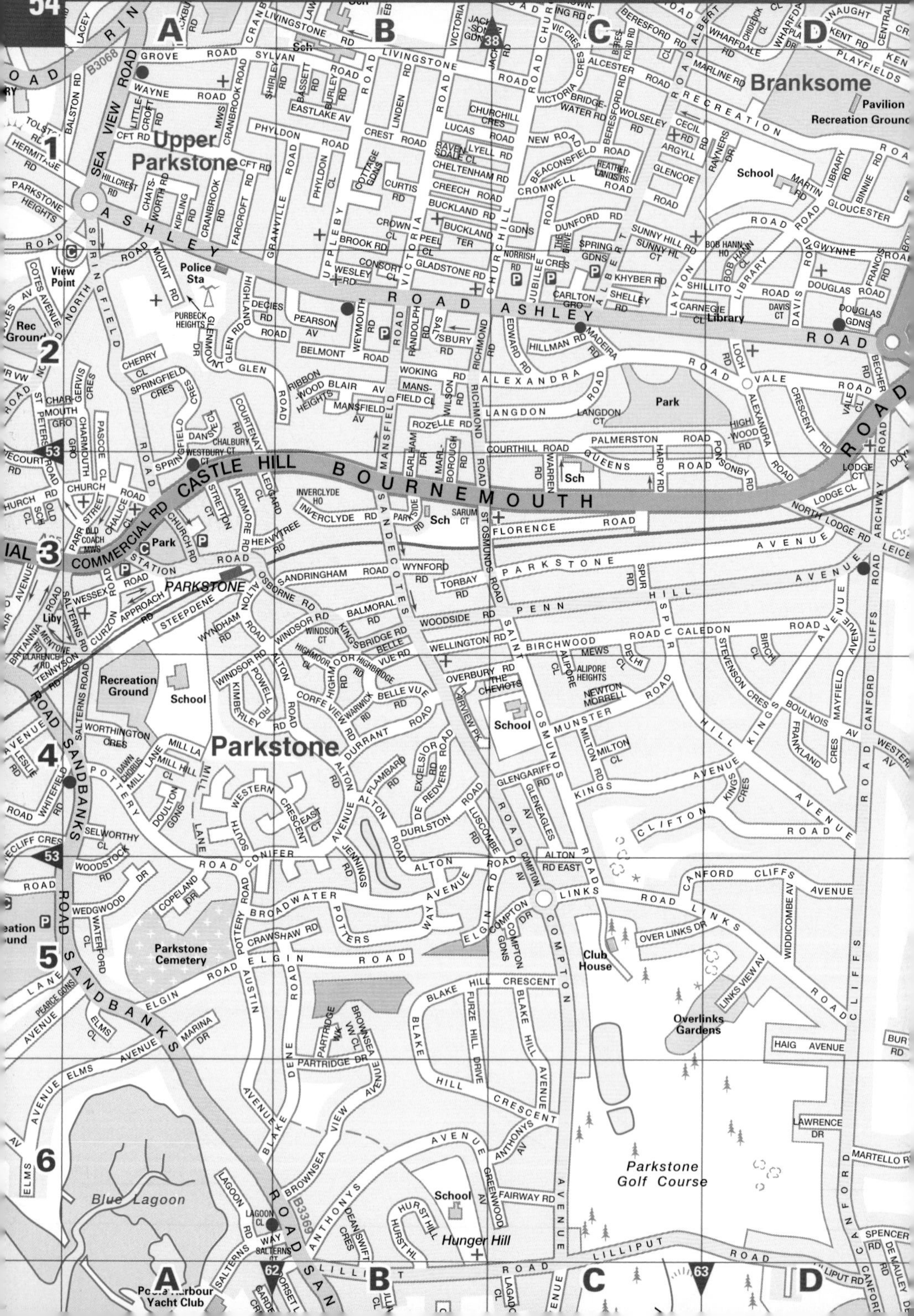
A
B
C
D
1
2
3
4
5
6
Upper Parkstone
Parkstone
Branksome
Pavilion
Recreation Ground
School
Library
Park
Sch
Police Sta
View Point
Rec Ground
Recreation Ground
Parkstone Cemetery
Club House
Overlinks Gardens
Parkstone Golf Course
Hunger Hill
Blue Lagoon
Poole Harbour Yacht Club
PARKSTONE
B3068
B3369
38
53
62
63
ASHLEY ROAD
BOURNEMOUTH ROAD
CASTLE HILL
COMMERCIAL RD
SANDBANKS ROAD
LILLIPUT ROAD
CANFORD CLIFFS ROAD
PENN HILL AVENUE
PARKSTONE AVENUE
SEA VIEW ROAD
GROVE ROAD
WAYNE ROAD
LIVINGSTONE RD
PHYLDON ROAD
CREST ROAD
CHURCHILL CRES
LUCAS ROAD
CHELTENHAM RD
CREECH ROAD
BUCKLAND RD
GLADSTONE RD
ALEXANDRA ROAD
LANGDON ROAD
PALMERSTON ROAD
COURTHILL ROAD
QUEENS ROAD
FLORENCE ROAD
SANDRINGHAM ROAD
STATION ROAD
WOODSIDE RD
WELLINGTON RD
BIRCHWOOD MEWS
CALEDON ROAD
MUNSTER ROAD
KINGS AVENUE
CLIFTON ROAD
LINKS ROAD
ALTON ROAD
DURRANT ROAD
BROADWATER AVENUE
POTTERY ROAD
ELGIN ROAD
CONIFER AVENUE
ELMS AVENUE
BROWNSEA VIEW AVENUE
BLAKE HILL CRESCENT
HAIG AVENUE
MARTELLO RD
ALBERT RD
RECREATION ROAD
GLOUCESTER ROAD
DOUGLAS ROAD
VALE ROAD
NORTH LODGE RD
ARCHWAY ROAD

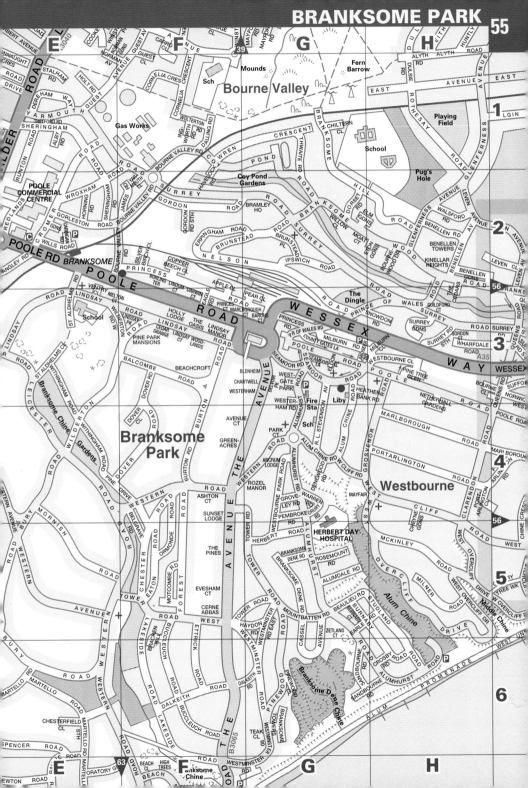

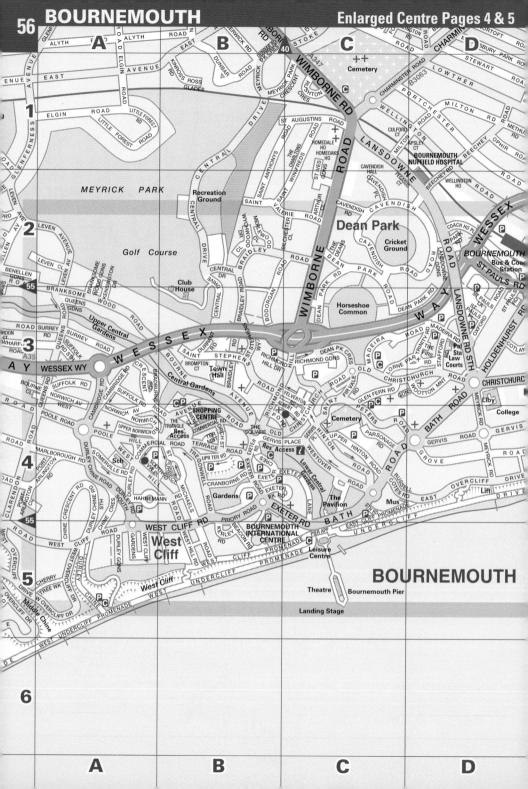

Boscombe

Boscombe Pier

Poole   Bay

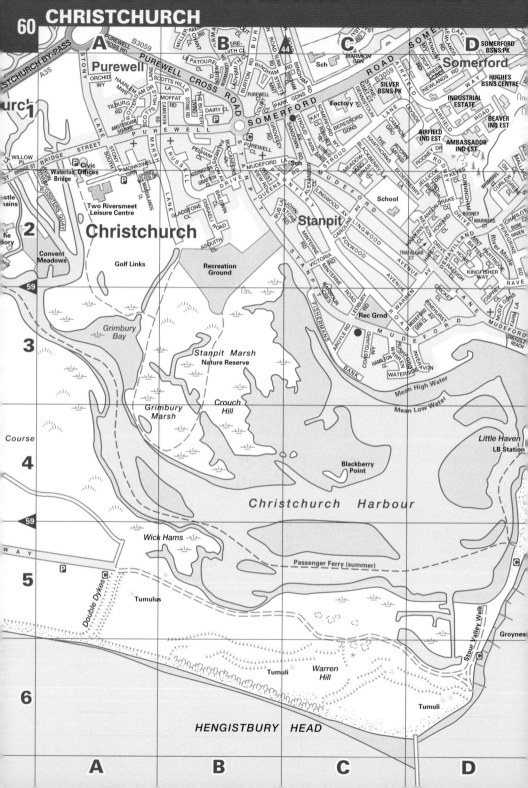

CHRISTCHURCH

Purewell

Somerford

Christchurch

Stanpit

Two Riversmeet
Leisure Centre

Civic
Offices

Waterloo
Bridge

Convent
Meadows

Golf Links

Recreation
Ground

Grimbury
Bay

Stanpit Marsh
Nature Reserve

Grimbury
Marsh

Crouch
Hill

Blackberry
Point

Christchurch Harbour

Course

Little Haven
LB Station

Wick Hams

Passenger Ferry (summer)

Double Dykes

Tumulus

Stour Valley Walk

Groynes

Tumuli

Warren
Hill

Tumuli

HENGISTBURY HEAD

SILVER
BSNS PK

HUGHES
BSNS CENTRE

INDUSTRIAL
ESTATE

AIRFIELD
IND EST

AMBASSADOR
IND EST

BEAVER
IND EST

Factory

School

Sch

Sch

Mean High Water

Mean Low Water

Rec Grnd

Club House

Golf Course

HIGHCLIFFE CASTLE
CP

Nature Reserve

ROTHESAY DR

47

AUCKLAND RD

WELLINGTON

AVENUE

Friars Cliff

High Cliff

PENNY WY

Groynes

PROMENADE

Mudeford

Caravan Park

Sandhills

The Run

Christchurch Bay

E   F   G   H

1

2

3

4

5

6

Poole Harbour Yacht Club

Salterns Point

Marina

Lilliput

CRICHEL MNT RD

Landing Stages

HARBOUR WATCH

LITTLE CT

MINTERNE GRANGE

ALLINGTON HO

HONEYWOOD HO

ALINGTON HO

ALINGTON CL

MOUNT GRACE DR

SHORE ROAD

ROAD

Pier

M a i n   C h a n n e l

Passenger Ferry (summer only)

The Villa

Nature Reserve

Brownsea Island
(National Trust)

Harley Wood

Church Hill

BRANKSEA CASTLE

Farm Buildings

Piers

Brownsea Island Ferry

Harry Point

North Haven Point

Stone Island

Piers

Landing Stages

OLD COASTGUARD RD

GIN ALLEY

THE HORSESHOE

GRASMERE

SEACOMBE

BROWNSEA

PANORAMA

SALTER ROAD

RD

Landing Stages

Recreation Ground

PROMENADE

BANKS ROAD

ROAD

ROAD

BANKS ROAD

Groyne

Sandbanks

SANDBANKS BSNS CENTRE

PANORAMA RD

BANKS RD

FERRY WY

Hotel

CARINA CT

MIDWAY PATH

Vehicular Ferry

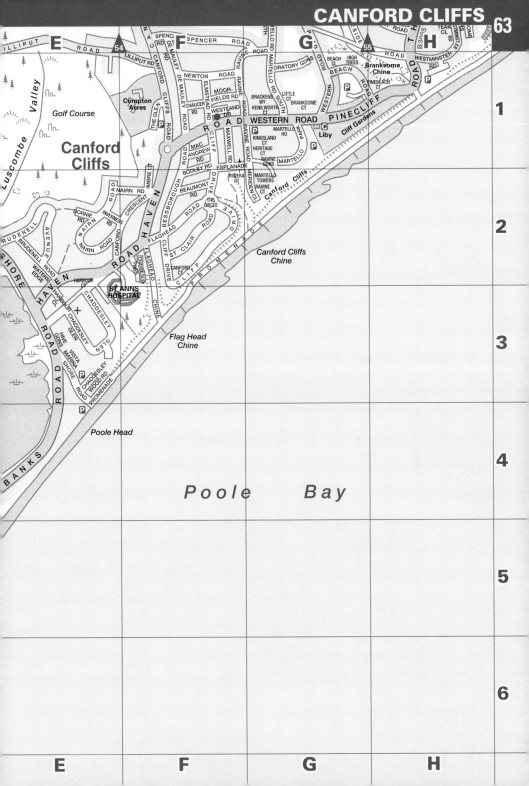

Poole Bay

Canford Cliffs

Golf Course

Luscombe Valley

Compton Acres

Canford Cliffs Chine

Flag Head Chine

Poole Head

Branksome Chine

Canford Cliffs Chine

St Anns Hospital

E   **F**   **G**   **H**

1   2   3   4   5   6

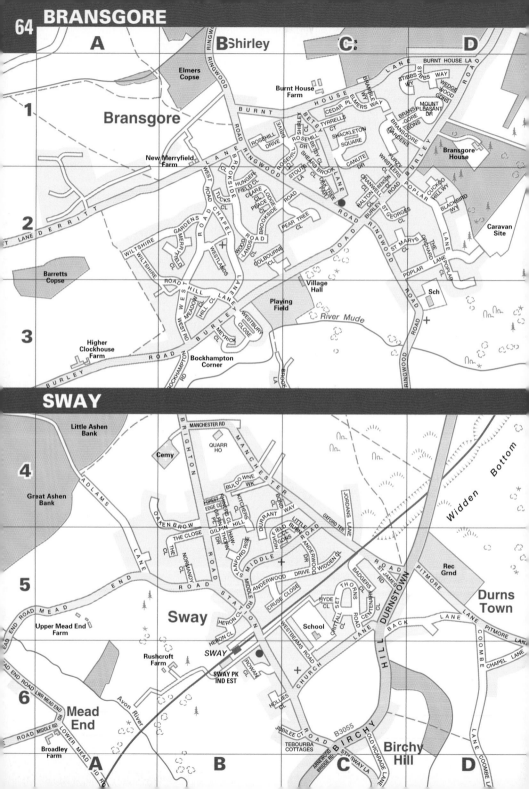

The Index includes some names for which there is insufficient space on the maps. These names are indicated by an * and are followed by the nearest adjoining thoroughfare.

Aaron Cl BH17 37 G5
Abbey Gdns BH21 22 C3
Abbey Rd BH22 14 C6
Abbots Cl BH23 47 A7
Abbotsbury Rd BH18 28 A6
Abbott Cl BH9 40 D5
Abbott Rd BH9 40 D5
Abbott St BH21 20 A2
Abbotts Way BH22 14 D6
Aberdare Rd BH10 40 B1
Abingdon Dr BH23 47 D7
Abingdon Rd BH7 37 F4
Abinger Rd BH7 58 B2
Abney Rd BH10 40 A1
Acacia Av BH31 7 E4
Acacia Rd SO41 50 B1
Acland Rd BH9 40 D5
**Acorn Bsns Pk
BH12 38 A4**
Acorn Cl,
  Christchurch BH23 43 F6
Acorn Cl,
  New Milton BH25 48 D3
Acorn Cl,
  Ringwood BH24 15 G3
Acorn Cotts BH31 7 B1
Acorn Mews BH23 60 C1
Acorn Way BH31 7 C2
Acres Rd BH11 39 G2
Acton Rd BH10 39 G3
Adamsfield Gdns
  BH10 39 G2
Adastral Rd BH17 37 F5
Adastral Sq BH17 37 G5
Addington Ct SO41 51 D2
Addington Pl BH23 60 B2
Addiscombe Rd BH23 43 G6
Addison Sq BH24 18 D5
Adelaide Cl BH23 43 F5
Adelaide La BH1 4 D3
Adelaide Rd BH9 6 D2
Adeline Rd BH5 57 G3
Adlams La SO41 64 A4
Admirals Walk BH2 4 B5
Admiralty Rd BH6 59 F5
Agarton La SO41 51 F1
Aggis Farm BH31 7 B2
Airetons Ct BH18 37 E2
**Airfield Ind Est
BH23 60 D1**
Airfield Rd BH23 60 D1
Airfield Way BH23 60 C1
Airspeed Rd BH23 61 E1
Akeshill Cl BH25 48 C2
Alan Ct BH23 47 C7
Albany Cl BH23 49 B6
Albany Dr BH21 8 A4
Albany Gdns BH15 52 A5
Albany Pk BH17 36 D5
Albemarle Rd BH3 40 C6
Albert Rd,
  Bournemouth BH1 4 D3
Albert Rd,
  Ferndown BH22 23 H3
Albert Rd,
  New Milton BH25 48 B4
Albert Rd, Poole BH12 54 C2
Albert Rd,
  Wimborne BH21 27 F5
Albion Cl BH12 38 A6
Albion Rd BH23 43 F5
Albion Way BH31 7 A2
Alby Rd BH12 55 E1
Alcester Rd BH12 54 C1
Aldbury Ct BH25 49 B8
Alder Cl BH23 44 A4
Alder Cres BH12 39 E5
Alder Heights BH12 39 E6
Alder Hills BH12 39 F5
**Alder Hills Ind Est
BH12 39 E5**
Alder Rd BH12 39 E6
Alderley Rd BH10 32 A6
Alderney Av BH12 38 C3
Aldis Gdns BH15 52 A4

Aldridge Rd,
  Bournemouth BH10 31 H6
Aldridge Rd,
  Ferndown BH22 24 B5
Aldridge Way BH22 24 B5
Alexander Cl BH23 60 C2
Alexandra Lodge BH1 5 E4
Alexandra Rd,
  Bournemouth BH6 58 C3
Alexandra Rd,
  Poole BH14 54 B2
Alexandria Cl BH14 24 A4
Alford Rd BH3 40 A6
Alington Cl BH14 62 D2
Alington Rd,
  Bournemouth BH3 40 C6
Alington Rd,
  Poole BH14 54 C3
Alipore Cl BH14 54 C3
Alipore Heights BH14 54 C4
Allen Ct BH21 20 D3
Allen Rd BH21 21 E5
Allenby Cl BH17 36 D3
Allenby Rd BH17 36 D3
Allens La BH16 34 F4
Allens Rd BH16 34 F4
Allenview Rd BH21 20 D3
Allington Ho BH14 62 D2
Alma Rd BH9 40 B5
Almer Rd BH15 35 F6
Almond Gro BH12 38 C5
Alpine Rd BH24 16 C6
Alton Rd,
  Bournemouth BH10 39 F4
Alton Rd, Poole BH14 54 A3
Alton Rd East BH14 54 C5
Alum Chine Rd BH4 55 G4
Alum Prom BH13 55 G6
Alumdale Rd BH4 55 G5
Alumhurst Rd BH4 55 G4
Alverton Av BH15 53 G3
Alyth Rd BH3 40 A6
Ambassador Cl BH23 61 E1
**Ambassador Ind Est
BH23 60 D1**
Amber Rd BH21 27 D6
Amberley Cl BH23 47 A6
Amberley Ct BH1 5 F4
Amberwood BH22 24 B2
Amberwood Cl BH23 47 B5
Amberwood Dr BH23 47 B5
Amberwood Gdns
  BH23 47 B5
Ambleside Rd BH23 42 D2
Ambury La BH23 44 C5
Amesbury Rd BH6 58 C2
Amethyst Rd BH23 44 C6
Ameys La BH23 24 C2
Ameysford Rd BH22 13 G5
Amira Ct BH2 4 C3
Ampfield Rd BH8 41 F1
Amsterdam Sq BH23 60 A1
Anchor Cl,
  Bournemouth BH11 31 E5
Anchor Cl,
  Christchurch BH23 31 E5
Anchor Rd BH11 31 E5
Ancrum Lodge BH13 55 G4
Anderwood Dr SO41 64 B5
Andover Cl BH23 45 F6
Andrew La BH25 48 E4
Andrews Cl BH11 39 F1
Androse Gdns BH24 18 C5
Angel La,
  Ferndown BH22 23 G6
Angel La,
  New Milton BH25 49 E7
Angeline Cl BH23 47 A6
Anjou Cl BH11 30 D5
Annandale Ct BH6 58 D4
Anne Cl BH23 43 G5
Annerley Rd BH1 5 H2
Annett Cl BH15 52 A4
Anson Cl,
  Christchurch BH23 60 D2
Anson Cl,
  Ringwood BH24 19 F3
Anstey Cl BH11 31 F5
Anstey Rd BH11 31 E6
Anthonys Av BH14 54 B6
Antler Dr BH25 48 A3
Anvil Cres BH18 28 A6
Apollo Cl BH12 38 C5
Apple Cl BH12 55 F2

Apple Gro BH23 43 E4
Apple Tree Gro BH22 24 B3
Appleslade Way BH25 48 C2
Appletree Cl,
  Bournemouth BH6 58 C2
Appletree Cl,
  New Milton BH25 49 C6
Approach Rd BH14 54 A3
April Cl BH11 31 F6
Apsley Cres BH17 36 D3
Apsley Ct BH8 56 D1
Aragon Way BH9 33 E6
Arcadia Av BH8 41 E5
Arcadia Rd BH23 43 F5
Archdale Cl BH10 40 A3
Archway Rd BH14 54 D3
Arden Rd BH9 40 C1
Arden Walk BH25 48 D4
Ardmore Rd BH14 54 A3
Arena Way BH21 30 A4
Argyle Rd BH23 60 C3
Argyll Mansions BH5 57 G3
Argyll Rd,
  Bournemouth BH5 57 G3
Argyll Rd, Poole BH12 54 C1
Ariel Cl BH6 59 G3
Ariel Dr BH6 59 G3
Ark Dr BH22 24 B5
Arley Rd BH14 53 H4
Arlington Ct BH25 49 C7
Arne Av BH12 38 D5
Arne Cres BH12 38 D5
Arne View Cl BH16 34 D3
Arnewood Ct BH2 4 B5
Arnewood Rd BH6 58 C3
Arnold Rd BH22 14 A3
Arnold Rd BH22 14 A4
Arnolds Cl BH25 49 A7
Arran Way BH23 47 C6
Arrowsmith La BH21 29 F3
Arrowsmith Rd BH21 29 E5
Arthur Cl BH2 4 D1
Arthur La BH23 59 G1
Arthur Rd BH23 59 G1
Arundel Cl BH25 46 F4
Arundel Way BH23 47 A8
Ascham Rd BH8 57 E2
Ascot Rd BH18 28 B6
Ash Cl BH16 34 D2
Ash Gro,
  Lymington SO41 50 A5
Ash Gro,
  Ringwood BH24 19 E5
Ashbourne Ct BH1 5 H4
Ashbourne Rd BH5 58 B3
Ashbrook Walk BH16 34 A3
Ashburn Garth BH24 19 F5
Ashburton Gdns BH10 40 A3
Ashdene Cl BH21 21 F3
Ashdown BH2 4 A5
Ashdown Cl BH17 37 G4
Ashdown Walk BH25 49 D5
Ashford Rd BH6 42 D6
Ashington Gdns BH21 28 B2
Ashington La BH21 20 C6
Ashington Pk BH25 49 D5
Ashleigh Rise BH10 40 A3
Ashlet Gdns BH25 48 E3
Ashley Arnewood Ct*,
  Ashley Rd BH25 48 D4
Ashley Cl,
  Ringwood BH24 19 F5
Ashley Common Rd
  BH25 48 D2
Ashley Dr North BH24 15 H1
Ashley Dr South BH24 15 H1
Ashley Dr West BH24 15 H1
**Ashley Heath Ind Est
BH21 9 E5**
Ashley La,
  Lymington SO41 50 A1
Ashley La,
  New Milton BH25 48 E3
Ashley Meads BH25 48 E3
Ashley Pk BH24 16 A1
Ashley Rd,
  Bournemouth BH1 57 G1
Ashley Rd,
  New Milton BH25 48 C4
Ashley Rd, Poole BH14 54 A1
Ashling Cl BH8 41 E4
Ashling Cres BH8 41 E4

Ashmeads Cl BH21 22 A2
Ashmeads Way BH21 21 H2
Ashmore Av,
  New Milton BH25 49 C6
Ashmore Av,
  Poole BH14 52 B6
Ashmore Cres BH15 52 B5
Ashmore Gro BH23 45 H4
Ashridge Av BH10 32 A5
Ashridge Gdns BH10 32 A5
Ashton Ct BH13 55 F4
Ashton Rd BH9 40 B2
Ashtree Cl BH25 48 E4
Ashurst Rd,
  Bournemouth BH8 41 F1
Ashurst Rd,
  Ferndown BH22 14 A3
Ashwell Ct BH23 44 A5
Ashwood Dr BH18 29 E6
Aspen Dr BH31 7 E2
Aspen Gdns BH12 39 E5
Aspen Pl BH25 49 C6
Aspen Rd BH12 39 E5
Aspen Way BH12 39 E5
Asquith Cl BH23 60 B2
Astbury Av BH12 39 E4
Aston Mead BH23 43 E2
Athelney Ct BH1 5 H4
Athelstan Rd BH6 59 E3
Aubrey Cl SO41 51 F3
Auckland Rd BH23 45 F6
Audemer Ct BH24 19 E4
Austen Av BH10 32 A6
Auster Cl BH23 61 E1
Austin Av BH14 54 A5
Austin Cl BH1 57 F1
Autumn Cl BH22 23 G1
Autumn Copse BH25 48 E4
Autumn Rd BH11 38 C1
Avalon BH14 62 C1
Avebury Av BH10 32 A5
Avenue Ct BH13 55 F4
Avenue La BH2 4 C4
Avenue Rd,
  Bournemouth BH2 4 C4
Avenue Rd,
  Christchurch BH23 43 F6
Avenue Rd,
  New Milton BH25 48 B4
Avenue Rd,
  Walkford BH23 47 D5
Avenue Rd,
  Wimborne BH21 27 F5
Aviation Pk BH23 33 F2
Avon Av BH24 16 D5
Avon Bldgs BH23 59 G1
Avon Castle Dr BH24 16 D5
Avon Causeway BH23 17 B5
Avon Cl BH8 57 F1
Avon Ho BH9 4 B5
Avon Mews BH8 41 E6
Avon Pk BH24 16 D1
Avon Rd,
  Bournemouth BH8 41 E6
Avon Rd,
  Ferndown BH22 14 B5
Avon Rd East BH23 43 G6
Avon Rd West BH23 43 F6
Avon Run Cl BH23 61 E3
Avon Run Rd BH23 61 E3
**Avon Trading Pk
BH23 43 G6**
Avon View Par BH24 44 A3
Avon View Rd BH23 43 H3
Avon Wharf BH23 60 A1
Avoncliffe Rd BH6 58 D4
Award Rd BH21 23 E4
Axford Cl BH8 41 G1
Aylesbury Rd BH1 57 G2
Aysha Cl BH25 49 C5
Azalea Cl BH24 16 A3
Azura Cl BH21 8 D6

Back La,
  Lymington SO41 64 C5
Back La,
  Ringwood BH24 19 F5
Badbury Cl BH18 37 E1
Badbury View Rd BH21 26 F2
Badbury Vw BH21 21 E3
Bader Cl BH25 49 D5
Bader Rd BH17 37 F5
Badger Way BH31 7 C3

Badgers Cl,
  Lymington SO41 64 C5
Badgers Cl,
  Ringwood BH24 16 A2
Badgers Copse BH25 48 D1
Badgers Walk BH22 24 B1
Bailey Cl BH25 48 E3
Bailey Cres BH15 37 E6
Bailey Dr BH23 59 F1
Baiter Gdns BH15 6 C5
Baker Rd BH11 31 E5
Bakers Farm Rd BH31 7 B1
Balcombe Rd BH13 55 F3
Baldwin Cl BH23 60 B2
Balena Cl BH17 36 C4
Balfour Cl BH23 45 G5
Balfour Rd BH9 40 C1
Ball La BH15 6 B5
Ballam Cl BH16 34 E3
Ballard Cl,
  New Milton BH25 48 C3
Ballard Cl, Poole BH15 6 C5
Ballard Rd BH15 53 E6
Balmoral Av BH8 41 H3
Balmoral Cl BH23 47 C8
Balmoral Ho BH2 4 A3
Balmoral Rd BH14 54 B3
Balmoral Walk BH25 48 A4
Balston Rd BH14 54 A1
Balston Ter BH15 6 B4
Banbury Rd BH17 37 E5
Bank Cl BH23 59 H1
Banks Rd BH13 62 C6
Bankside Rd BH9 40 D2
Banstead Rd BH18 28 C5
Barberry Way BH31 7 F3
Barbers Gate BH15 6 A5
Barbers Gate*,
  Thames St BH15 52 D5
Barbers Piles BH15 6 A5
Barbers Piles*,
  West Quay Rd BH15 52 D5
Barbers Wharf BH15 6 A5
Barclay Mansions BH2 4 D1
Bargates BH23 59 G1
Baring Rd BH6 59 F4
Barlands Cl BH23 44 A3
Barn Cl BH16 34 C3
Barn Rd BH18 36 D2
Barnes Cl BH10 40 A2
Barnes Cres,
  Bournemouth BH10 40 A2
Barnes Cres,
  Wimborne BH21 21 F4
Barnes La SO41 51 D1
Barnes Rd BH10 40 A2
Barnfield BH23 45 G6
Barns Rd BH22 24 C2
Barnsfield Rd BH24 16 A6
Barnsley Dro BH21 10 A4
Barons Cl BH12 55 G3
Barons Rd BH11 30 C4
Barrack Rd,
  Christchurch BH23 42 D6
Barrack Rd,
  Ferndown BH22 32 D2
Barrie Rd BH9 40 C2
Barrington Ct BH3 40 A5
Barrow Dr BH8 41 H3
Barrow Rd BH8 41 H3
Barrow Vw BH22 23 F2
Barrow Way BH8 41 H2
Barrowgate Rd BH8 41 F1
Barrowgate Way BH8 41 F1
Barrs Av BH25 48 C3
Barrs Wood Dr BH25 48 C3
Barrs Wood Rd BH25 48 D3
Barry Gdns BH18 28 B5
Barter Rd BH12 39 F5
Barters La BH18 36 B1
Bartlett Dr BH7 42 B6
Bartley Ct BH21 20 D3
Barton Cft BH25 49 B7
Barton Common La
  BH25 49 C8
Barton Common Rd
  BH25 49 C8
Barton Court Av BH25 49 B6
Barton Court Rd BH25 49 B6
Barton Dr BH25 49 A7
Barton Grn BH25 49 C8
Barton Ho BH25 47 F8
Barton La BH25 47 F6
Barton Way BH25 49 A7

Barton Wood Rd BH25 49 A8
Bartonside Rd BH25 47 D7
Bascott Cl BH11 39 F3
Bascott Rd BH11 39 E3
Bashley Cross Rd,
  Christchurch BH23 46 C3
Bashley Cross Rd,
  New Milton BH25 48 A2
Bashley Dr BH25 48 C1
Bashley Rd BH25 48 B1
Bassett Rd BH12 54 B1
Batchelor Cres BH11 39 E1
Batchelor Rd BH11 39 E1
Batcombe Cl BH11 38 D1
Bath Cl BH1 5 F4
Bath Rd BH1 5 E5
Batstone Way BH22 23 G2
Batten Cl BH23 44 B6
Baverstock Rd BH12 39 G5
Bay Cl, Poole BH16 34 D4
Bay Cl, Wimborne BH21 8 B4
Bay Hog La BH15 6 A4
Bay Tree Way BH23 45 H4
Beach Av BH25 49 A8
Beach Cl BH13 63 G1
Beach Rd,
  Branksome Pk BH13 63 G1
Beach Rd, Upton BH16 34 C3
Beachcroft BH23 55 F3
Beacon Cl SO41 50 A5
Beacon Dr BH23 47 A8
Beacon Dr BH23 47 A7
Beacon Gdns BH18 36 A2
Beacon Hill La BH21 27 C7
Beacon Park Cres BH16 34 C2
Beacon Park Rd BH16 34 C2
Beacon Rd,
  Bournemouth BH2 4 C5
Beacon Rd,
  Broadstone BH18 36 A2
Beacon Rd,
  Poole BH14 34 C2
Beacon Way BH18 27 F7
Beaconsfield Rd,
  Christchurch BH23 59 H1
Beaconsfield Rd,
  Poole BH12 54 C1
Beamish Rd BH17 37 G4
Bear Cross BH11 31 E4
Bear Cross Av BH11 30 D4
Beatty Cl BH24 19 F3
Beatty Rd BH9 40 D3
Beauchamp Pl BH23 43 G6
Beauchamps Gdns
  BH8 42 A5
Beaucroft La BH21 21 F2
Beaucroft Rd BH21 21 F2
Beaufort Cl BH23 61 F1
Beaufort Dr BH21 21 E3
Beaufort Rd BH6 58 C3
Beaufoys Av BH22 23 H2
Beaufoys Cl BH22 23 H2
Beaufoys Ct BH22 23 H2
Beaulieu Av BH23 43 E6
Beaulieu Cl BH25 46 F4
Beaulieu Rd,
  Bournemouth BH4 55 G5
Beaulieu Rd,
  Christchurch BH23 43 E6
Beaver Ind Est
  BH23 60 D1
Beccles Cl BH15 52 B5
Becher Rd BH14 54 C4
Beckhampton Rd BH15 52 A3
Beckley Copse BH23 47 C5
Becton La BH25 49 C8
Becton Mead BH25 49 C6
Bedale Way BH15 53 G1
Bedford Cres BH7 42 C6
Bedford Rd North
  BH12 38 B2
Bedford Rd South
  BH12 38 B3
Beech Av,
  Bournemouth BH6 58 C4
Beech Av,
  Christchurch BH23 42 D5
Beech Cl,
  Broadstone BH18 36 A1
Beech Cl,
  Lymington SO41 50 A5
Beech Cl, Verwood BH31 7 A3
Beech Ct BH21 21 F4
Beech La BH24 15 G4
Beech Wood Dr BH18 36 C1
Beechbank Av BH17 36 A4
Beechcroft La BH24 18 D3
Beechey Rd BH8 56 D2

Beechwood Av,
  Bournemouth BH5 57 H3
Beechwood Av,
  New Milton BH25 48 A3
Beechwood Ct BH2 14 C6
Beechwood Gdns BH5 58 A3
Beechwood Rd BH22 14 C6
Belben Cl BH12 38 C2
Belben Rd BH12 38 B2
Belfield Rd BH6 59 G4
Belgrave Ct BH1 57 F3
Belgrave Rd BH13 55 F4
Bell Heather Cl BH16 34 D2
Belle Vue Cl BH6 58 D4
Belle Vue Cres BH6 59 F4
Belle Vue Gdns BH6 59 F4
Belle Vue Gro BH22 14 B4
Belle Vue Mansions
  BH6 59 E4
Belle Vue Rd,
  Bournemouth BH6 58 D4
Belle Vue Rd,
  Poole BH14 54 B3
Belle Vue Walk BH22 24 A6
Bellflower Cl BH23 45 E5
Bells Ho BH21 21 E2
Belmont Av BH8 41 F2
Belmont Cl BH31 7 C3
Belmont Rd,
  New Milton BH25 48 E3
Belmont Rd,
  Poole BH14 54 B2
Belvedere Rd,
  Bournemouth BH3 40 D6
Belvedere Rd,
  Christchurch BH23 59 G1
Belvoir Pk BH13 55 G3
Bemister Rd BH9 40 C4
Benbow Cres BH12 38 D3
Benbridge Av BH11 31 E5
Bendigo Rd BH23 43 E5
Benellen Av BH4 55 H2
Benellen Gdns BH4 4 A2
Benellen Rd BH4 55 H2
Benellen Towers BH4 55 H2
Bengal Rd BH9 40 B4
Benjamin Rd BH15 35 F7
Benmoor Rd BH17 36 B5
Benmore Cl BH25 49 E5
Benmore Rd BH9 40 C4
Bennett Rd BH8 41 E6
Bennetts Alley BH15 6 B5
Bennion Rd BH10 39 G2
Benridge Cl BH18 36 C1
Benson Cl BH23 64 C2
Benson Rd BH17 37 E5
Bentley Rd BH9 40 C1
Bere Cl BH17 37 E2
Beresford Cl BH12 54 C1
Beresford Gdns BH23 60 C1
Beresford Rd,
  Bournemouth BH6 58 C3
Beresford Rd,
  Poole BH12 54 C1
Berkeley Av BH12 38 C4
Berkeley Cl BH31 7 B1
Berkeley Ct*,
  Moorside Rd BH22 14 A5
Berkeley Rd BH3 40 B5
Berkley Av BH22 24 A6
Bermuda Ct BH23 47 B7
Bernards Cl BH23 43 E6
Berne Ct BH1 5 F4
Berrans Av BH11 31 F5
Berryfield Rd SO41 50 C3
Bertram Rd BH25 48 D3
Berwick Rd BH3 40 B6
Berwyn Ct BH18 28 C6
Bessborough Rd BH23 63 F2
Bessemer Cl BH31 7 F4
Beswick Av BH10 40 A2
Bethany Ho BH1 57 F2
Bethia Cl BH8 41 G6
Bethia Rd BH8 41 F6
Betsy Cl BH23 64 C1
Betsy La BH23 64 C1
Bettiscombe Cl BH17 37 F2
Beverley Gdns BH10 40 A1
Bexington Cl BH11 38 D1
Bickerley Gdns BH24 18 C5
Bickerley Rd BH24 18 B5
Bickerley Ter BH24 18 B5
Bicton Rd BH11 39 G2
Bindon Cl BH12 38 D6
Bingham Av BH14 62 D1
Bingham Cl,
  Christchurch BH23 60 C1
Bingham Cl,
  Verwood BH31 7 D4
Bingham Dr BH31 7 D4

Bingham Rd,
  Bournemouth BH9 40 C5
Bingham Rd,
  Christchurch BH23 60 B1
Bingham Rd,
  Verwood BH31 7 D4
Binnie Rd BH12 54 D1
Birch Av,
  Christchurch BH23 43 H3
Birch Av,
  Ferndown BH22 32 B1
Birch Cl,
  New Milton BH25 46 F1
Birch Cl, Poole BH14 54 D3
Birch Cl,
  Ringwood BH24 15 G3
Birch Cl,
  Wimborne BH21 26 E4
Birch Dr BH8 42 A3
Birch Gro,
  Ferndown BH22 14 A4
Birch Gro,
  New Milton BH25 49 C6
Birch Rd BH24 16 B3
Birch Walk BH22 24 B5
Birchdale Rd BH21 21 F3
Birchwood Cl BH23 45 H5
Birchwood Mews BH14 54 C4
Birchwood Rd,
  Parkstone BH14 54 C3
Birchwood Rd,
  Upton BH16 34 D3
Birchy Hill SO41 64 C6
Birds Hill Gdns BH15 53 F3
Birds Hill Rd BH15 53 F3
Birkdale Ct BH18 28 C5
Birkdale Rd BH18 28 C5
Bishop Cl BH12 39 G6
Bishop Ct BH24 18 D4
Bishop Rd BH9 40 D4
Bishops Cl BH7 41 H6
Bitterne Way BH31 7 C3
Black Hill BH31 7 D2
Black Moor Rd BH31 7 F4
Blackberry La BH23 60 C1
Blackbird BH17 36 A4
Blackbird Way BH23 64 D2
Blackburn Rd BH12 38 A6
Blackbush Rd SO41 51 C2
Blackfield La BH22 14 B3
Blackfield Rd BH8 41 F4
Blacksmith Cl BH21 27 F5
Blackthorn Way,
  New Milton BH25 48 E3
Blackthorn Way,
  Verwood BH31 7 E3
Blackwater Dr BH21 29 E3
Blair Av BH14 54 B2
Blair Cl BH25 48 A4
Blake Dene Rd BH14 54 A6
Blake Hill Av BH14 54 C5
Blake Hill Cres BH14 54 B5
Blandford Cl BH15 52 B5
Blandford Ct SO41 51 D2
Blandford Rd,
  Corfe Mullen BH21 26 D1
Blandford Rd,
  Poole BH15,16 34 D3
Blandford Rd,
  Wimborne BH21 20 A1
Blandford Rd North
  BH16 27 A6
Blaney Way BH21 26 E4
Blenheim BH13 55 G3
Blenheim Cres SO41 50 A1
Blenheim Dr BH23 61 E1
Blind La BH21 20 D3
Bloomfield Av BH9 40 C2
Bloomfield Pl BH9 40 C2
Bloxworth Rd BH12 39 E4
Bluebell Cl BH23 45 F6
Bluebell La BH17 36 A4
Blyth Cl BH23 42 D2
Blythe Rd BH21 26 E4
Blythswood Ct BH25 49 B7
Bob Hann Cl BH12 54 D2
Bob Hann Ho BH12 54 D1
Bockhampton Rd,
  Bransgore BH23 64 B3
Bockhampton Rd,
  Christchurch BH23 44 A1
Bodley Rd BH13 63 F2
Bodorgan Rd BH2 4 D2
Bodowen Cl BH23 44 A4
Bodowen Rd BH23 44 A4
Bognor Rd BH18 28 B6
Boldre Cl,
  New Milton BH25 47 E7
Boldre Cl, Poole BH12 38 D6
Boleyn Cres BH9 33 E6

Bolton Cl BH6 59 E5
Bolton Cres BH22 24 C2
Bolton Rd BH6 59 E5
Bond Av BH22 14 A3
Bond Cl SO41 64 B4
Bond Rd BH15 53 G1
Bonham Rd BH9 40 B5
Bonington Cl BH23 44 B6
Border Dr BH16 34 E4
Border Rd BH16 34 E4
Boreham Rd BH6 58 D2
Borley Rd BH17 36 B5
Borthwick Rd BH1 57 G2
Boscombe Cliff Rd
  BH5 57 H3
Boscombe Grove Rd
  BH1 57 F1
Boscombe Overcliff Dr
  BH5 57 G4
Boscombe Prom BH5 57 G4
Boscombe Spa Rd
  BH5 57 G3
Bosley Cl BH23 43 E4
Bosley Way BH23 43 E4
Bosworth Mews BH9 33 E6
Boulnois Av BH14 54 D4
Boundary Dr BH21 21 E2
Boundary La BH24 15 F5
Boundary Rd BH10 40 A5
Bountys La BH12 54 D1
Bourne Av BH2 4 B3
Bourne Cl BH2 4 A3
Bourne Ct,
  Bournemouth BH2 4 D3
Bourne Ct,
  Wimborne BH21 21 E3
Bourne Pines BH1 5 E1
Bourne Valley Rd BH12 55 E2
**Bournemouth Central
  Bsns Pk BH1 57 E2**
Bournemouth Rd BH14 54 B3
Bourneview Ct BH2 4 C3
Bournewood Dr BH4 55 H2
Bourton Gdns BH7 42 B6
Bouverie Cl BH25 49 B6
Boveridge Gdns BH9 33 E6
Bovington Cl BH17 37 H3
Bowden Rd BH12 38 B2
Bower Rd BH8 41 F4
Bowland Rise BH25 48 D4
Box Cl BH17 36 C5
Boyd Rd BH12 39 E6
Brabazon Dr BH23 61 E1
Brabazon Rd BH21 29 H1
Brabourne Av BH22 23 H4
Bracken Cl,
  Bournemouth BH6 58 C4
Bracken Rd,
  Ferndown BH22 23 F1
Bracken Way BH23 47 C6
Brackendale Cl BH21 8 A4
Brackendale Rd BH8 41 F4
Brackenhill BH13 55 F6
Brackenhill Rd BH21 22 A1
Brackens Way BH13 63 G1
Brackley Cl BH23 17 A4
Bradburne Rd BH2 4 B3
Bradford Rd BH9 41 F1
Bradpole Rd BH8 41 G3
Bradstock Cl BH12 39 E4
Braemar Av BH6 59 G4
Braemar Cl BH6 59 G4
Braemar Dr BH23 47 A6
Braeside,
  Ferndown BH22 14 B3
Braeside Rd,
  Ringwood BH24 15 G2
Braidley Rd BH2 4 C3
Brailswood Rd BH15 53 F2
Braishfield Gdns BH8 41 G2
Bramble Cl BH23 14 A4
Bramble La BH23 47 C6
Bramble Way BH23 64 C1
Bramley Cl BH22 23 H2
Bramley Ho BH12 55 G2
Bramley Rd,
  Bournemouth BH10 31 G5
Bramley Rd,
  Ferndown BH22 23 H2
Brampton Rd BH15 37 F6
Bramshaw Gdns BH8 41 G2
Bramshaw Way BH25 47 E6
Branders Cl BH6 59 G3
Branders La BH6 59 G3
Branksea Av BH15 52 A6
Branksea Cl BH15 52 A6
Branksome Bsns Pk
  BH21 21 G5

Branksome Dene Rd
  BH4 55 G5
Branksome Hill Rd BH4 55 G1
Branksome Towers
  BH13 55 G6
Branksome Wood Gdns
  BH2 4 A2
Branksome Wood Rd
  BH4 4 A2
Bransgore Gdns BH23 64 C1
Branwell Cl BH23 44 A3
Branwood Cl SO41 50 B5
Brassey Cl BH9 40 C3
Brassey Rd BH9 40 C3
Brassey Ter BH9 40 C3
Braxton Courtyard
  SO41 50 B6
Breach La BH24 19 G4
Breamore Cl BH25 48 A4
Brecon Cl,
  Bournemouth BH10 32 B4
Brecon Cl,
  New Milton BH25 49 D5
Bredy Rd BH17 37 F3
Bremble Cl BH12 38 C2
Briar Cl,
  Christchurch BH23 60 C2
Briar Cl, Poole BH15 53 G3
Briar Way BH21 22 A3
Briarswood Rd BH16 34 E3
Brickyard La,
  Corfe Mullen BH21 26 C2
Brickyard La,
  Verwood BH31 7 A1
Brickyard La,
  Wimborne BH21 23 F2
Bridge App BH15 6 A5
Bridge Pl BH10 32 A4
Bridge St BH23 59 H2
Bridges Rd BH22 14 D3
Bridgewater Rd BH12 54 C1
Bridle Cl BH16 34 F3
Bridle Cres BH7 42 C6
Bridle Way BH21 22 A2
Bridleways BH31 7 A3
Bridport Rd,
  Poole BH12 39 E4
Bridport Rd,
  Verwood BH31 7 C3
Brierley Av BH22 32 B1
Brierley Cl BH10 32 B6
Brierley Rd BH10 32 A6
Bright Rd BH15 53 F1
Brightlands Av BH22 59 F3
Brighton Rd SO41 64 B4
Brinsons Cl BH23 44 A3
Brisbane Rd BH23 43 E5
Britannia Rd BH14 53 H4
Britannia Way BH23 61 E1
Brixey Cl BH12 38 B5
Brixey Rd BH12 38 B6
Broad Av BH8 41 G4
Broad Mead Rd BH11 31 E3
Broadfields Cl SO41 51 E2
Broadhurst Av BH10 32 A6
Broadlands Av BH6 59 F3
Broadlands Cl,
  Bournemouth BH8 41 G1
Broadlands Cl,
  Christchurch BH23 47 D5
Broadmayne Rd BH12 39 E5
Broadmoor Rd BH21 26 D4
Broadshard Ct BH24 18 D3
Broadshard La BH24 18 D3
Broadstone Way
  BH15,17,18 28 D4
Broadwater Av BH14 54 A5
Broadway BH6 59 F3
Broadway Gdns BH9 21 E4
Broadway La BH8 41 E2
Brock Way BH31 7 B1
Brockenhurst Rd BH9 41 E3
Brockhills La BH25 48 D2
Brockley Rd BH10 40 A1
Brocks Pine BH24 15 H3
Brockwood BH24 15 F4
Brog St BH21 26 E1
Brompton Ct BH2 4 C4
Bronte Av BH23 43 F5
Brook Av BH25 48 C3
Brook Av North BH25 48 C2
Brook Cl BH10 39 H1
Brook Dr BH31 7 E4
Brook La,
  Christchurch BH23 64 B3
Brook La,
  Wimborne BH21 26 E4
**Brook Pk Ind Est
  BH21 21 G5**

Brook Rd,
  Bournemouth BH10   31 G6
Brook Rd, Poole BH12   54 B1
Brook Rd,
  Wimborne BH21   21 F4
Brook Way BH23   61 F1
Brookdale Cl BH18   28 C6
Brookdale Farm BH18   28 C6
Brooklyn Ct BH25   48 B4
Brookside Cl BH23   64 B2
Brookside Rd,
  Christchurch BH23   64 B1
Brookside Rd,
  Wimborne BH21   21 G4
Brookside Way BH23   47 A5
Broom La BH8   58 C3
Broom Rd BH12   38 C3
Broomfield Ct BH22   24 B3
Broughton Av BH10   40 A1
Broughton Cl BH10   40 B1
Brownen Rd BH9   40 D5
Browning Av BH5   58 A3
Browning Rd BH12   54 B1
Brownsea Av BH21   26 F4
Brownsea Cl BH25   48 A4
Brownsea Rd BH13   62 C5
Brownsea View Av
  BH14   54 B6
Brownsea View Cl
  BH14   54 B5
Brudenell Av BH13   63 E2
Brudenell Rd BH13   63 E2
Brune Way BH22   24 A6
Brunel Cl BH31   7 F4
Brunstead Pl BH12   55 G2
Brunstead Rd BH12   55 F2
Brunswick Ho BH2   4 B3
Bryanstone Rd BH3   40 B5
Bryant Rd BH12   39 F5
Bryony Cl BH18   36 A2
Bub La BH23   60 B2
Buccaneers Cl BH23   60 B1
Buccleuch Rd BH13   55 F5
Bucehayes Cl BH23   64 D4
Buchanan Av BH7   41 G6
Buckingham Ct BH23   47 B7
Buckingham Mansions
  BH1   5 F3
Buckingham Rd BH12   38 C6
Buckingham Walk
  BH25   48 A4
Buckland Gro BH23   45 H4
Buckland Rd BH12   54 A1
Buckland Ter BH17   47 B7
Bucklers Way BH8   41 G1
Buckstone Cl SO41   50 B4
Buckthorn Cl BH17   36 A3
Buddens Mdw BH21   26 E6
Buffalo Mews BH15   52 D5
Buffalo Mews*,
  Market BH15   52 D5
Bugdens La BH31   7 C2
Buldowne Walk SO41   64 B4
Bull La BH15   6 B5
Bullfinch Cl BH17   36 B3
Bunting Rd BH22   23 G1
Burbridge Cl BH17   37 G5
Burcombe Rd BH10   31 G6
Burcombe La BH24   19 G2
Burdock Cl BH23   45 F5
Bure Cl BH23   61 F2
Bure Haven Dr BH23   60 D2
Bure Homage Gdns
  BH23   61 E2
Bure Homage La BH23   61 E2
Bure Pk BH23   61 E3
Bure Rd BH23   61 F1
Bure Rd BH23   61 F2
Burford Cl BH23   42 D5
Burford Ct BH1   5 H3
Burgess Cl BH17   31 E6
Burleigh Rd BH6   58 C2
Burley Cl,
  New Milton BH25   47 E7
Burley Cl,
  Verwood BH31   7 B3
Burley Rd,
  Bransgore BH23   64 A3
Burley Rd,
  Christchurch BH23   44 A1
Burley Rd, Poole BH12   54 B1
Burling Ter BH12   55 F2
Burlington Arc BH1   5 E3
Burn Cl BH31   7 E4
Burnaby Ct BH4   55 G5
Burnaby Rd BH4   55 G5
Burnbake Rd BH31   7 C3
Burnbrae Rd BH22   32 A1
Burnett Av BH23   43 E6

Burnett Rd BH23   43 F6
Burngate Rd BH15   52 A4
Burnham Dr BH8   41 F5
Burnham Rd BH23   43 H3
Burnleigh Gdns BH25   48 E3
Burns Rd BH6   58 D1
Burnside BH23   45 G6
Burnt House La BH23   64 B1
Burtley Rd BH6   59 E4
Burton Cl,
  Christchurch BH23   44 A5
Burton Cl,
  Ringwood BH24   15 G1
Burton Grn BH23   44 A3
Burton Hall BH23   44 A3
Burton Hall Pl BH23   44 A3
Burton Rd,
  Christchurch BH23   44 B6
Burton Rd, Poole BH13   55 F4
Burtoncroft BH23   44 A5
Burts Hill BH21   20 D2
Bury Rd BH13   54 D5
Bushell Rd BH15   36 D6
Bushey Rd BH8   41 E4
Bushmead Dr BH24   15 G1
Bute Dr BH23   47 C7
Butlers La BH24   19 E3
Buttercup Dr BH23   45 E5
Buttons La BH15   6 B5
Buttons La*,
  Strand St BH15   52 D5
Byron Cl BH22   24 A3
Byron Rd,
  Bournemouth BH5   57 H3
Byron Rd,
  New Milton BH25   47 F6
Byron Rd,
  Wimborne BH21   21 E3

Cabot La BH17   36 C5
Cabot Way BH25   48 A4
Cadhay Cl BH25   48 A4
Cadnam Way BH8   41 G1
Cadogan Ct BH1   5 H3
Cadogan Rd BH24   18 D4
Caesars Way BH18   28 A6
Caird Av BH25   48 D4
Cairns Cl BH23   43 F5
Caister Cl BH22   23 H2
Calder Rd BH17   37 G4
Caledon Rd BH14   54 C3
Caledonian Cl BH23   61 F1
Calkin Cl BH23   43 G5
Calluna Rd BH12   38 A4
Calmore Cl BH8   41 F1
Calvin Rd BH9   40 C4
Cambridge Gdns BH23   43 A4
Cambridge Rd BH2   4 A4
Camden Cl BH9   40 D3
Camden Hurst SO41   51 B3
Camellia Cl BH1   8 A3
Camellia Gdns BH25   48 C4
Cameron Rd BH23   60 B1
Cammel Rd BH22   24 A6
Campbell Rd,
  Bournemouth BH1   57 G2
Campbell Rd,
  Christchurch BH23   43 H3
Campion Gro BH23   60 C1
Canberra Rd BH23   43 E5
Candys Cl BH21   20 A6
Candys La BH21   20 A6
Canford Av BH11   39 E3
Canford Bottom BH21   22 A2
Canford Cliffs Av BH14   54 C5
Canford Cliffs Rd BH13   54 D6
Canford Cres BH13   63 E2
Canford Ct BH13   63 F2
Canford Gdns BH11   39 F3
Canford Heath Rd
  BH17   37 E3
Canford Magna BH21   29 H2
Canford Park Av BH21   30 A3
Canford Rd,
  Bournemouth BH11   39 F4
Canford Rd, Poole BH15   6 D1
Canford View Dr BH21   22 B2
Canford Way BH12   38 A2
Cannon Cl BH18   36 B3
Cannon Hill Gdns BH21   22 A1
Cannon Hill Rd BH21   22 A1
Canons Walk SO41   51 E2
Canterbury Cl BH22   14 B6
Canute Dr BH23   64 C1
Capella Ct BH2   4 D5
Capesthorne BH23   61 E3
Capstone Pl BH8   57 F1
Capstone Rd BH8   40 D6
Caradon Pl BH31   7 A1
Carbery Av BH6   58 D3

Carbery Gdns BH6   59 E3
Carbery La*,
  Carbery Row BH6   58 C4
Carbery Row BH6   58 C3
Cardigan Rd,
  Bournemouth BH9   40 B5
Cardigan Rd,
  Poole BH12   55 E2
Carey Rd BH9   40 B2
Careys Rd BH8   41 F1
Carina Ct BH13   62 C6
Carisbrooke Cres BH15   35 F6
Carisbrooke Ct,
  Christchurch BH23   47 C7
Carisbrooke Ct,
  New Milton BH25   48 A4
Carisbrooke Way BH23   45 H5
Carlton Av BH25   47 H5
Carlton Gate BH4   4 A6
Carlton Gro BH12   54 C2
Carlton Rd BH1   57 F2
Carlyle Rd BH6   58 D1
Carmel Cl BH15   35 F7
Carnarvon Rd BH1   57 G2
Carnegie Cl BH12   54 C2
Caroline Av BH23   60 C2
Caroline Rd BH11   39 G2
Carradale BH23   45 F6
Carrbridge Cl BH3   39 H6
Carrbridge Gdns BH3   39 H6
Carrbridge Rd BH3   39 H6
Carrick Way BH25   48 B5
Carrington Av BH23   51 F3
Carrington La SO41   51 F3
Carroll Av BH22   24 A3
Carroll Cl BH12   39 H3
Carsworth Way BH17   37 H2
Carters Av BH15   35 F6
Carters La BH15   6 B4
Cartref Cl BH31   7 C2
Cartwright Cl BH10   31 H6
Carvers La BH24   18 C5
Carysfort Rd BH1   57 G2
Cashmoor Cl BH12   39 E5
Caslake Cl BH25   49 B6
Cassel Av BH13   55 G6
Casterbridge Rd BH22   23 G5
Castle Av BH23   47 A7
Castle Cl SO41   51 E4
Castle Gate Cl BH8   41 F3
Castle Hill BH14   54 A3
Castle La East BH8   42 A5
Castle La West BH8,9   40 D1
Castle Par BH7   42 D6
Castle Rd BH9   40 C3
Castle St,
  Christchurch BH23   59 H2
Castle St, Poole BH15   6 B4
Castledene Cres BH14   53 H4
Castlemain Av BH6   58 C3
Castleman Cl BH22   14 A4
Castleman Way BH24   18 C5
Castlemews BH21   16 C2
Castleton Av BH10   32 A4
Castlewood Rd BH24   16 D2
Catalina Cl BH23   61 E1
Catalina Dr BH15   53 F5
Caton Cl BH12   39 G5
Cattistock Rd BH8   41 G3
Cavan Cres BH17   36 D3
Cavendish Corner
  Caravan Pk BH24   19 E3
Cavendish Hall BH1   56 C1
Cavendish Pl BH1   56 C2
Cavendish Rd BH1   5 E1
Caversham Cl BH15   52 A4
Cawdor Rd BH3   40 A6
Caxton Cl BH23   44 D6
Cecil Av BH8   41 E5
Cecil Cl BH21   28 A5
Cecil Ct BH8   41 E5
Cecil Hill BH8   41 E5
Cecil Rd,
  Bournemouth BH5   57 G3
Cecil Rd, Poole BH12   54 C1
Cedar Av,
  Bournemouth BH10   32 A5
Cedar Av, C
  hristchurch BH23   42 D5
Cedar Av,
  Ringwood BH24   15 G3
Cedar Cl BH16   34 C2
Cedar Dr,
  Lymington SO41   50 A5
Cedar Dr,
  Wimborne BH21   22 A4
Cedar Gdns BH25   49 A6

Cedar Grange BH13   55 F3
Cedar Pk BH21   23 E2
Cedar Pl BH23   64 C1
**Cedar Trading Pk
  BH21   23 E2**
Cedar Way BH22   13 H6
Celandine Cl BH23   45 F6
Cellars Farm Rd BH6   59 G5
Cemetery Av BH15   53 G1
Cemetery Rd BH21   20 C3
Centenary Cl SO41   64 C5
Centenary Ho BH21   59 G1
Centenary Way BH1   57 G2
Central Av, Poole BH12   38 D6
Central Av,
  Wimborne BH21   26 F3
Central Dr BH2   4 C1
Centre La SO41   50 B4
Centre Pl BH24   18 B4
Cerne Abbas BH13   55 F5
Cerne Cl BH9   32 D6
Cerne Ct BH6   58 D4
Chaddesley Glen BH13   63 E3
Chaddesley Pines
  BH13   63 F2
Chaddesley Wood Rd
  BH13   63 E3
Chaffey Cl BH24   19 F4
Chaffinch Cl,
  New Milton BH25   48 A4
Chaffinch Cl, Poole BH17   36 B3
Chalbury Cl BH17   38 A3
Chalbury Ct BH14   54 A2
Chaldecott Gdns BH10   39 H1
Chaldon Rd BH17   37 H2
Chalfont Av BH23   42 D2
Chalice Cl BH4   54 A3
**Chalwyn Ind Est
  BH12   37 H5**
Champion Cl SO41   51 F3
Chander Cl BH22   24 A4
Chandlers Cl BH17   37 F1
Chandos Av BH12   39 F4
Channel Ct,
  Bournemouth BH6   58 D4
Channel Ct,
  New Milton BH25   47 F8
Chant Cl BH23   44 B6
Chantry Cl BH23   47 A5
Chapel Cl BH21   27 E5
Chapel Gate BH23   33 E2
Chapel La,
  Bransgore BH23   64 B2
Chapel La,
  Corfe Mullen BH21   27 D5
Chapel La,
  Lymington SO41   64 D6
Chapel La, Parley BH23   33 E1
Chapel La, Poole BH15   6 B4
Chapel La,
  Wimborne BH21   20 D3
Chapel Rd BH14   53 H3
Chapel Rise BH24   16 D5
Charborough Rd BH18   36 C1
Charing Cl BH24   18 D2
Charles Cres BH25   48 D2
Charles Gdns BH10   39 H2
Charles Keightley Ct
  BH21   21 F5
Charles Rd,
  Christchurch BH23   44 C5
Charles Rd, Poole BH15   6 D1
Charlotte Cl,
  Christchurch BH23   60 D2
Charlotte Cl,
  Poole BH12   39 G5
Charlton Cl,
  Bournemouth BH9   41 E1
Charlton Cl,
  Lymington SO41   50 A2
Charminster Av BH9   40 D3
Charminster Cl BH9   41 E3
Charminster Pl BH9   41 E3
Charminster Rd BH8   41 E4
Charmouth Gro BH14   54 A2
Charnock Cl SO41   50 D2
Charnwood Av BH9   40 D1
Charnwood Cl BH22   14 B4
Charter Rd BH11   30 C5
Chartwell BH13   55 G3
Chase Cl BH31   7 F3
Chaseside BH7   42 A6
Chatsworth Rd,
  Bournemouth BH8   41 E6
Chatsworth Rd,
  Poole BH15   54 A1
Chatsworth Way BH25   46 F4
Chaucer Cl BH21   20 D2
Chaucer Dr SO41   51 D3

Chaucer Rd BH13   63 F1
Chaucombe Pl BH25   49 A6
Cheam Rd BH18   28 B6
Cheddington Rd BH9   40 D1
Chedington Cl BH17   37 F3
Chelmsford Rd BH16   34 C3
Cheltenham Rd BH12   54 B1
Chene Rd BH21   21 F4
Cherford Rd BH11   39 G2
Cherita Ct BH15   53 G1
Cheriton Av BH7   42 C6
Cheriton Way BH21   21 E2
Cherrett Cl BH11   31 E6
Cherries Dr BH9   40 B3
Cherry Cl BH14   54 A2
Cherry Gro BH22   23 H2
Cherry Hill Gro BH16   34 D4
Cherry Tree Cl,
  Lymington SO41   50 B5
Cherry Tree Cl,
  Ringwood BH24   15 G3
Cherry Tree Ct*,
  Station Rd BH25   49 C5
Cherry Tree Dr BH25   46 F2
Cherry Tree Walk BH4   4 A6
Cheshire Dr BH8   42 A4
Chesilbourne Gro BH8   41 F2
Chesildene Av BH8   41 F2
Chesildene Dr BH8   41 F1
Chessel Av BH5   58 A4
Chester Rd BH13   55 F5
Chesterfield Cl BH13   55 F6
Chesterfield Ct BH1   57 F4
Chestnut Av,
  Bournemouth BH6   58 C3
Chestnut Av,
  Christchurch BH23   42 D5
Chestnut Av,
  New Milton BH25   49 B7
Chestnut Gro BH21   22 D3
Chestnut Way BH23   43 H2
Chetnole Cl BH17   37 H3
Chetwode Way BH17   36 D3
Cheviot Cl BH23   44 C5
Cheviot Way BH31   7 C3
Chewton Common Rd
  BH23   47 B6
Chewton Farm Rd
  BH23   47 C7
Chewton Lodge BH23   47 C7
Chewton Way BH23   47 C6
Cheyne Gdns BH4   55 H5
Chichester Rd BH24   19 F3
Chichester Walk BH21   29 G1
Chichester Way BH23   61 E3
Chickerell Cl BH9   40 D1
Chideock Ct BH12   38 D6
Chigwell Rd BH8   41 E4
Chilcombe Rd BH6   58 C2
Chilfrome Cl BH17   37 E3
Chiltern Cl,
  Bournemouth BH4   55 G1
Chiltern Cl,
  New Milton BH25   49 A6
Chiltern Ct*,
  Hunt Rd BH23   44 D5
Chiltern Dr,
  New Milton BH25   47 F6
Chiltern Dr,
  Verwood BH31   7 C2
Chine Cres BH2   4 B5
Chine Crescent Rd BH2   4 B5
Chine Walk BH22   24 B6
Chiswell Rd BH17   37 E3
Chloe Gdns BH12   38 C5
Chorley Cl BH15   37 E6
Chris Cres BH16   34 D3
Christchurch Bay Rd
  BH25   49 A8
Christchurch By-Pass
  BH23   44 A6
Christchurch Rd,
  Bournemouth BH1,7   5 G3
Christchurch Rd,
  Ferndown BH22   31 G1
Christchurch Rd,
  Hurn BH23   17 B5
Christchurch Rd,
  Lymington SO41   50 A5
Christchurch Rd,
  New Milton BH25   49 A6
Christchurch Rd,
  Ringwood BH24   18 C5
Christopher Cres BH15   36 D6
Church Hill,
  Lymington SO41   51 E3
Church Hill,
  Verwood BH31   7 B2

Church La,
Bournemouth BH8 42 B2
Church La,
Christchurch BH23 59 H2
Church La,
Ferndown BH22 32 B4
Church La,
Lymington SO41 64 C6
Church La,
New Milton BH25 49 A5
Church Rd,
Bournemouth BH6 59 E4
Church Rd,
Ferndown BH22 23 H2
Church Rd, Poole BH14 53 H3
Church Rd,
Wimborne BH21 8 A3
Church St,
Christchurch BH23 59 H2
Church St, Poole BH15 6 A5
Church St,
Wimborne BH21 20 D4
Churchfield BH31 7 B2
Churchfield Cres BH15 53 G3
Churchfield Ct BH15 53 F4
Churchfield Rd BH15 53 F4
Churchill Cres BH12 54 B1
Churchill Ct BH25 49 A5
Churchill Gdns BH12 54 C1
Churchill Rd,
Bournemouth BH1 57 G2
Churchill Rd,
Poole BH12 38 C6
Churchill Rd,
Wimborne BH21 21 F5
Churchmoor Rd BH21 21 H3
Cinnamon La BH15 6 B5
Claire Ct BH23 47 B7
Clare Lodge Cl BH23 64 B2
Claremont Av BH9 40 D3
Claremont Rd BH9 41 E3
Clarence Park Rd BH7 58 A2
Clarence Rd BH14 53 H4
Clarence Pl BH23 43 F5
Clarence Rd BH14 53 H4
Clarendon Cl BH18 28 C6
Clarendon Rd,
Bournemouth BH4 4 A4
Clarendon Rd,
Broadstone BH18 36 A1
Clarendon Rd,
Christchurch BH23 43 G6
Clarks Cl BH24 18 C5
Clayford Av BH22 23 G1
Clayford Cl BH17 37 E3
Claylake Dr BH31 7 D3
Cleeves Cl BH12 38 C2
Clematis Cl BH23 45 F5
Cleveland Cl BH25 47 F7
Cleveland Ct B42 4 A5
Cleveland Gdns BH1 57 F1
Cleveland Rd BH1 57 F1
Cliff Cres BH25 49 A8
Cliff Dr,
Christchurch BH23 61 F2
Cliff Dr, Poole BH13 63 F1
Cliff Ho BH6 59 E5
Cliff Rd SO41 51 A2
Cliff Ter BH25 49 A8
Cliffe Rd BH25 47 F7
Clifford Rd BH9 40 D3
Clifton Gdns BH22 23 H5
Clifton Rd,
Bournemouth BH6 58 D4
Clifton Rd, Poole BH14 54 C4
Clingan Rd BH6 58 D1
Clinton Cl BH23 47 C5
Clive Rd,
Bournemouth BH9 40 C4
Clive Rd,
Christchurch BH23 45 H4
Cliveden Cl BH22 23 H1
Cloughs Rd BH24 18 D4
Clover Cl BH23 45 F5
Clover Ct,
Christchurch BH23 45 F5
Clover Dr,
New Milton BH25 48 E3
Clover Dr BH17 36 B4
Clowes Av BH6 59 G5
Clyde Rd BH17 36 D3
Coach House Mews
BH22 24 B1
Coach House Pl BH1 5 F1
Coastguard Cotts BH25 47 F7
Coastguard Way BH23 60 C3
Cobbs La BH15 37 F6
Cobbs Quay BH15 52 A3
Cobbs Rd BH21 21 F2
Cobham Rd,
Bournemouth BH9 40 D1

Cobham Rd,
Ferndown Ind Est
BH21 13 F6
Cobham Rd,
Wimborne BH21 29 G1
Cockerell Cl BH21 29 G1
Cogdean Cl BH21 28 A2
Cogdean Walk BH21 28 A2
Cogdean Cl BH21 28 A2
Cogdeane Rd BH17 37 E2
Colborne Av BH21 21 G3
Colborne Cl BH15 6 D4
Colbourne Cl BH23 64 B2
Colehill Cres BH9 40 D1
Colehill La BH21 21 G2
Coleman Rd BH11 39 F2
Colemere Gdns BH23 47 A6
Colemore Rd BH7 42 C6
Coleridge Grn BH23 44 D6
Coles Av BH15 52 A5
Coles Gdns BH15 52 A5
Colin Cl BH21 27 F5
College Rd,
Bournemouth BH5 58 A4
College Rd,
Ringwood BH24 18 C5
Collingbourne Av BH6 58 D1
Collingwood Rd BH21 14 B1
Collins La BH24 18 C4
Collwood Cl BH15 37 E6
Colman Ct BH1 57 F3
Colonnade Rd BH6 58 A3
Colonnade Rd West
BH5 58 A3
Colt Cl BH21 22 B2
Columbia Rd BH10 39 G2
Columbia Trees La
BH10 39 G3
Columbian Way BH10 39 H3
Columbine Cl BH23 45 E5
Colville Cl BH5 58 A3
Colville Rd BH5 58 A3
Comber Rd BH9 40 C1
Comet Way BH23 61 E1
Comley Rd BH9 40 B2
Commercial Rd,
Bournemouth BH2 4 B4
Commercial Rd,
Poole BH14 53 H3
Compton Av BH14 54 C4
Compton Beeches
BH24 16 A2
Compton Cl BH31 7 C2
Compton Cres BH22 14 D5
Compton Dr BH14 54 C5
Compton Gdns BH14 54 C5
Compton Rd BH25 49 B5
Condor Cl BH21 14 D1
Coneygar La BH22 23 F6
Conifer Av BH14 54 A5
Conifer Cl,
Christchurch BH23 42 D3
Conifer Cl,
Ferndown BH22 32 B1
Conifer Cl,
Ringwood BH24 15 F2
Coniston Av BH11 31 E5
Coniston Rd BH24 18 D5
Connaught Cl BH25 47 F6
Connaught Cres BH12 38 D6
Connaught Rd BH7 58 B2
Connell Rd BH15 52 D2
Consort Cl BH12 54 B2
Constable Cl BH22 23 H4
Constitution Hill Gdns
BH14 53 H1
Constitution Hill Rd
BH14 53 G2
Conway Cl BH25 48 D4
Conways Dr BH14 53 H2
Cook Cl BH24 19 E3
Cook Row BH21 20 D4
Cooke Gdns BH12 39 E6
Cooke Rd BH12 39 E6
Coombe Av BH10 40 A1
Coombe Gdns BH10 40 A2
Coombe La SO41 64 D5
Cooper Dean Dr BH8 42 A5
Coopercourt Leaze
BH21 21 E4
Coopers La BH31 7 B1
Copeland Dr BH14 54 A5
Copper Beech Cl BH12 55 F2
Copper Beech Gdns
BH10 40 A2
Coppice Av BH22 23 G1
Coppice Cl,
New Milton BH25 48 E3

Coppice Cl,
Ringwood BH24 15 H2
Copse Av BH25 49 C5
Copse Cl BH14 53 H4
Copse Rd,
New Milton BH25 48 C4
Copse Rd,
Verwood BH31 7 C2
Copse Way BH23 45 H6
Copsewood Av BH8 41 H4
Copythorne Cl BH8 41 F2
Corbar Rd BH23 43 E6
Corbiere Av BH12 38 C3
Corbin Av BH22 24 C2
Corfe Halt Cl BH21 28 A1
Corfe Lodge Rd BH18 27 F6
Corfe Mews BH15 53 F3
Corfe View Rd,
Poole BH14 54 B4
Corfe View Rd,
Wimborne BH21 27 E5
Corfe Way BH18 36 A2
Corhampton Rd BH6 58 B2
Corn Market BH21 20 D4
Cornelia Cres BH12 55 F1
Cornflower Dr BH23 45 F5
Cornford Way BH23 45 G6
Cornish Gdns BH10 39 H3
Cornwallis Rd SO41 51 C3
Coronation Av,
Bournemouth BH9 40 C3
Coronation Av,
Poole BH16 34 D2
Coronation Cl BH31 7 B1
Coronation Rd BH31 7 C1
Corporation Rd BH1 5 H1
Corscombe Cl BH17 37 F2
Cortry Cl BH12 39 E6
Cotes Av BH14 53 H2
Cotlands Rd BH1 5 G2
Cotswold Cl BH31 7 C3
Cotswold Ct*,
Hunt Rd BH23 44 D5
Cottage Gdns BH12 54 B1
Cottagers La SO41 50 B2
Cotton Cl BH18 28 B5
Countess Cl BH21 29 F2
Countess Gdns BH7 41 H5
County Gates La BH4 54 B5
Court Cl BH23 60 B1
Court Rd BH9 40 D3
Courtenay Dr BH21 21 E3
Courtenay Rd BH14 54 A2
Courthill Rd BH14 54 B3
Courtleigh Manor BH5 57 F3
Courtney Pl BH21 27 E5
Cove Rd BH10 39 H3
Covena Rd BH6 58 D2
Coventry Cl BH21 27 C6
Coventry Cres BH17 36 C3
Cowdrey Gdns BH8 42 A3
Cowdrys Fld BH21 20 D2
Cowell Dr BH7 42 A6
Cowgrove Rd BH21 20 A4
Cowley Rd BH17 37 F4
Cowleys Rd BH23 43 H3
Cowper Av BH25 49 B6
Cowper Rd BH9 40 B2
Cowpitts La BH21 19 F2
Cowslip Rd BH18 36 A3
Cox Av BH9 40 D1
Cox Cl BH9 40 D1
Coxstone La BH24 18 C5
Coy Pond Rd BH12 55 F1
Crab Orchard Way BH21 8 B2
Crabton Close Rd BH5 57 H3
Crabtree Cl BH23 44 A4
Craigmoor Av BH8 41 G3
Craigmoor Cl BH8 41 H3
Craigmoor Way BH8 41 H3
Craigside Rd BH24 15 G3
Craigwood Dr BH22 24 B4
Cranborne Cres BH12 38 D5
Cranborne Ct BH9 40 D4
Cranborne Pl BH25 48 A4
Cranborne Rd,
Bournemouth BH2 4 C5
Cranborne Rd,
Wimborne BH21 20 D2
Cranbrook Mews BH12 54 A1
Cranbrook Rd BH12 54 A1
Crane Cl BH31 7 B2
Crane Dr BH31 7 B2
Crane Way BH21 8 D6
Cranemoor Av BH23 45 H3
Cranemoor Cl BH23 45 H3
Cranemoor Gdns BH23 45 H3
Cranes Mews BH15 6 D2
Cranfield Av BH21 21 E3
Cranleigh Cl BH6 59 E3

Cranleigh Ct BH6 59 E3
Cranleigh Gdns BH6 59 E2
Cranleigh Rd BH6 58 D1
Cranmer Rd BH9 40 C5
Crantock Gro BH8 41 H3
Cranwell Cl,
Bournemouth BH11 30 D6
Cranwell Cl,
Christchurch BH23 64 C2
Crawshaw Rd BH14 54 A5
Creasey Rd BH11 31 F5
Creech Rd BH12 54 B1
Creedy Dr BH23 59 G2
Creedy Path BH23 59 G2
Creekmoor La BH17 36 B3
Crescent Cl BH25 49 A8
Crescent Dr BH25 49 A8
Crescent Rd,
Bournemouth BH2 4 B3
Crescent Rd,
Poole BH14 54 D2
Crescent Rd,
Verwood BH31 7 D2
Crescent Rd,
Wimborne BH21 21 E4
Crescent Walk BH22 32 B1
Crest Rd BH12 54 B1
Cresta Gdns BH22 24 B6
Cribb Cl BH17 37 G5
Crichel Mount Rd BH14 62 D1
Crichel Rd BH9 40 C5
Cricket Cl BH23 60 D2
Crimea Rd BH9 40 B5
Cringle Av BH6 59 G3
Crispin Cl BH23 47 A7
Crittall Cl SO41 64 C5
Crockford Cl BH25 48 C2
Croft Cl BH21 26 E4
Croft Rd,
Bournemouth BH9 40 B3
Croft Rd,
Christchurch BH23 60 D1
Croft Rd, Poole BH12 54 A1
Croft Rd,
Ringwood BH24 19 E2
Crofton Cl BH23 43 E5
Cromer Gdns BH12 55 E2
Cromer Rd,
Bournemouth BH8 41 F6
Cromer Rd,
Poole BH12 55 E2
Cromwell Pl BH5 58 B2
Cromwell Rd,
Bournemouth BH5 58 B3
Cromwell Rd,
Poole BH12 54 C1
Cromwell Rd,
Wimborne BH21 21 F4
Crooked La BH25 49 D7
Crosby Rd BH4 55 H6
Cross Way BH23 42 D4
Crossmead Av BH25 49 B5
Crossways SO41 50 A5
Crow Arch La BH24 18 D5
Crow Arch La Ind Est
BH24 18 D6
Crow Hill Ct BH15 53 F3
Crow La BH24 19 E6
Crown Cl BH12 54 B1
Crown Mead BH21 20 D4
Crusader Rd BH11 30 C6
Cruse Cl SO41 64 B5
Cucklington Gdns BH9 41 E1
Cuckoo Hill Way BH22 64 D2
Cuckoo Rd BH12 37 H5
Cudnell Av BH11 31 E4
Culford Cl BH8 41 H3
Culford Ct BH8 56 C1
Cull Cl BH12 39 H5
Cull La BH25 48 C1
Culliford Cres BH17 37 F2
Cullwood La BH25 48 D2
Culver Rd BH25 49 A5
Culverhayes Cl BH21 20 C3
Culverhayes Pl BH21 20 C3
Culverhayes Rd BH21 20 C2
Cumnor Rd BH1 5 F3
Cunningham Cl,
Bournemouth BH11 39 F1
Cunningham Cl,
Christchurch BH23 60 D2
Cunningham Cl,
Ringwood BH24 19 E3
Cunningham Cres BH11 39 F1
Cunningham Ct*,
Nelson Rd BH12 48 A4
Cunningham Pl BH11 39 F1
Curlew Cl BH23 23 G1
Curlew Rd,
Bournemouth BH8 41 F3

Curlew Rd,
Christchurch BH23 60 D2
Curlieu Rd BH15 37 F6
Curtis Rd BH12 54 B1
Curzon Rd,
Bournemouth BH1 57 F1
Curzon Rd, Poole BH14 54 A3
Curzon Way BH23 45 G6
Cuthburga Rd BH21 21 E4
Cuthbury Cl BH21 20 C4
Cuthbury Gdns BH21 20 C3
Cutler Cl,
New Milton BH25 48 C4
Cutler Cl, Poole BH12 39 H5
Cutlers Pl BH21 21 H3
Cynthia Cl BH12 38 A5
Cynthia Ho BH12 38 A5
Cynthia Rd BH12 38 A6
Cypress Gro SO41 51 B8
Cyril Rd BH8 57 E1

Dacombe Cl BH16 34 E3
Dacombe Dr BH16 34 E2
Dacres Walk SO41 51 E2
Dairy Cl, C
hristchurch BH23 60 B1
Dairy Cl,
Wimborne BH21 27 D6
Daisy La BH15 53 E1
Dakota Cl BH23 61 E1
Dale Cl BH15 37 G6
Dale Rd BH15 37 H6
Dale Valley Rd BH15 37 F6
Dales Cl BH21 22 B3
Dales Dr BH21 22 A3
Dales La BH23 33 G4
Dalewood Av BH11 30 D5
Dalkeith Arc BH1 5 E3
Dalkeith La BH1 5 E3
Dalkeith Rd BH22 23 H4
Dalling Rd BH21 27 F6
Dalmeny Rd BH6 59 F5
Damerham Rd BH8 41 G2
Dane Ct*,
St Peters Rd BH14 53 H2
Dane Dr BH22 24 B6
Dane Rd SO41 51 A1
Danecourt Cl BH14 53 G3
Danecourt Rd BH14 53 G3
Danecrest Rd SO41 50 A2
Danes Cl BH25 49 B7
Danesbury Av BH6 59 F3
Danesbury Mdws
BH25 48 D2
Danestream Cl SO41 51 E3
Danestream Ct SO41 51 E3
Daneswood Rd BH25 48 D4
Daniel Gdns BH15 6 C5
Daniel Gdns*,
Skinner St BH15 53 E5
Dansie Ct BH14 54 A4
Darbys Cl BH15 53 E1
Darbys Gdns BH15 37 E6
Darbys La North BH17 37 F5
Dark La,
Christchurch BH23 45 B3
Dark La,
New Milton BH25 48 A3
Darley Rd BH22 23 H5
Darracott Rd BH5 58 A3
Darrian Rd BH16 34 D3
Darwin Av BH23 43 E4
Darwin Cl BH12 55 F3
Davenport Cl BH16 34 E2
David Way BH15 35 F7
Davids La BH24 16 C2
Davis Ct BH12 54 D2
Davis Field BH25 49 A5
Davis Fld BH25 48 A4
Davis Rd BH12 54 D2
Dawkins Rd BH15 35 F6
Dawkins Way BH25 49 B5
Dawn Chorus BH14 54 A4
Dawn Cl BH10 39 H3
Daws Av BH11 39 F3
Daylesford Cl BH14 53 H5
Days Ct BH21 7 B1
De Courtenai Cl BH11 30 D6
De La Warr Rd SO41 51 C3
De Lisle Rd BH3 40 B6
De Mauley Rd BH3 63 F1
De Montfort Rd BH21 29 F2
De Redvers Rd BH14 54 B4
Deacon Gdns BH11 31 F6
Deacon Rd BH11 31 F6
Dean Cl BH15 52 A4

Dean Park Cres BH1 5 E3
Dean Park Rd BH1 5 E2
Dean Swift Cres BH14 54 B6
Deans Court La BH21 20 D4
Deans Ct SO41 51 E2
Deans Gro BH21 21 F1
Deans Rd BH5 58 B3
Deanscroft Rd BH10 40 B1
Deansleigh Rd BH7 42 B5
Dear Hay La BH15 6 B4
Decies Rd BH14 54 A2
Dee Way BH15 6 A4
Deepdene La BH11 30 D6
Deer Park Cl BH25 48 A3
Deerleap Way BH25 48 C1
DeHaviland Cl BH21 29 G1
DeHavilland Way BH23 60 D2
Delamere Gdns BH10 40 A2
Delft Mews*, Scotts Hills La BH23 60 A1
Delhi Cl BH14 54 C3
Delhi Rd BH9 40 B2
Delilah Rd BH15 35 F7
Dell Cl BH18 36 A1
Delph Rd BH21 29 E2
Delta Cl BH23 45 E6
Denby Rd BH15 53 F2
Dene Cl BH24 19 F2
Dene Walk BH22 32 B2
Deneve Av BH17 37 E3
Denewood Copse BH22 14 A3
Denewood Rd, Bournemouth BH4 55 G4
Denewood Rd, Ferndown BH22 14 A3
Denham Cl BH17 37 F2
Denham Dr BH23 47 A6
Denholm Cl BH24 19 F2
Denison Rd BH17 36 D3
Denmark La BH15 6 D2
Denmark Rd, Bournemouth BH9 40 C4
Denmark Rd, Poole BH15 6 C2
Denmead BH25 48 E3
Denmead Rd BH6 58 D1
Dennis Rd BH21 27 F5
Dennistoun Av BH23 60 C1
Derby Rd BH1 57 E3
Dereham Way BH12 55 E1
Derritt La BH23 64 A2
Derrybrian Gdns BH25 49 C5
Derwent Cl, Bournemouth BH9 40 C2
Derwent Cl, Ferndown BH22 24 D2
Derwent Rd BH25 48 C2
Derwentwater Rd BH21 21 E6
Deverel Cl BH23 43 G5
Devon Rd, Christchurch BH23 43 E6
Devon Rd, Poole BH15 53 G2
Deweys La BH24 18 B5
Dewlands Pk BH31 7 A2
Dewlands Rd BH31 7 A3
Dewlands Way BH31 7 A2
Dewlish Cl BH17 37 H2
Diana Cl BH22 24 A3
Diana Ct BH23 47 B7
Diana Way BH21 28 A3
Dibden Cl BH8 41 F1
Dickens Rd BH6 58 D1
Didcot Rd BH17 37 E5
Dilly La BH25 49 B7
Dingle Rd BH5 58 B4
Dingley Rd BH15 53 F1
Dinham Ct BH25 48 E3
Dinham Rd BH25 48 E3
Diprose Rd BH21 26 F3
Disraeli Rd BH23 60 B2
Doe Copse Way BH25 48 A3
Does La BH31 7 A2
Dogdean BH21 21 E1
Dogwood Rd BH18 36 A3
Dolbery Rd North BH12 38 C3
Dolbery Rd South BH12 38 C3
Dolphin Av BH10 32 A6
Dolphin Centre BH15 6 C3
Dolphin Pl BH25 49 B8
Dominion Rd BH11 38 D1
Donnelly Rd BH6 59 F3
Donnington Dr BH23 61 F1
Donoughmore Rd BH1 57 G2
Dorchester Gdns BH15 53 G1
Dorchester Mansions BH1 57 F3
Dorchester Rd, Poole BH15 53 E1
Dorchester Rd, Upton BH16 34 A3
Dornie Rd BH13 63 E2
Dorset Av BH22 23 H5
Dorset Lake Av BH14 62 C1
Dorset Rd, Bournemouth BH4 55 G2
Dorset Rd, Christchurch BH23 44 C6
Dorset Way BH17 37 E5
Douglas Av BH23 59 F2
Douglas Cl BH16 34 D2
Douglas Gdns BH12 54 D2
Douglas Mews, Bournemouth BH6 58 C3
Douglas Mews, Poole BH16 34 D2
Douglas Rd, Bournemouth BH6 59 E4
Douglas Rd, Poole BH12 54 D2
Doulton Gdns BH14 54 A4
Doussie Cl BH16 34 C2
Dover Cl BH13 55 F4
Dover Rd BH13 55 E4
Doveshill Cres BH10 40 A1
Doveshill Gdns BH10 40 A1
Dowlands Cl BH10 39 H1
Dowlands Rd BH10 39 H1
Downey Cl BH11 39 E3
Downlands Pl BH17 37 G5
Downton Cl BH8 41 F1
Downton La SO41 51 A2
Doyne Rd BH14 54 D3
Dragoon Way BH23 43 F6
Drake Cl, Christchurch BH23 60 D2
Drake Cl, New Milton BH25 48 A4
Drake Cl, Ringwood BH24 19 F3
Drake Ct BH15 6 B5
Drake Rd BH15 6 B5
Drakes Rd BH22 24 B5
Draper Rd, Bournemouth BH11 39 F1
Draper Rd, Christchurch BH23 44 B6
Draycott Rd BH10 40 A2
Dreswick Cl BH23 42 D2
Drew Cl BH12 39 G5
Droxford Rd BH6 58 B2
Druids Cl BH22 24 A6
Druitt Rd BH23 44 C6
Drummond Rd BH1 57 F2
Drury Rd BH4 55 G4
Dryden Cl BH24 15 G1
Dryden Pl SO41 51 D2
Duart Ct BH25 48 D4
Duck Island La BH24 18 C5
Duck La BH11 31 E6
Ducking Stool La BH23 59 H1
Dudley Av SO41 50 A3
Dudley Gdns BH10 32 A6
Dudley Pl*, Station Rd BH25 49 C5
Dudley Rd BH10 32 A6
Dudmoor Farm Rd BH23 43 F1
Dudmoor La BH23 43 E1
Dudsbury Av BH22 24 A4
Dudsbury Cres BH22 24 A4
Dudsbury Gdns BH22 32 B3
Dudsbury Rd BH22 24 A6
Dudsway Ct BH22 24 A4
Dugdell Cl BH22 24 C2
Dukes Cl BH6 58 D2
Dukes Dr BH11 30 D5
Dukesfield BH23 42 D4
Dulsie Rd BH3 39 H6
Dunbar Cres BH23 47 A5
Dunbar Rd BH3 56 B1
Duncan Rd BH25 48 E3
Duncliff Rd BH6 59 G3
Dundas Rd BH17 37 F5
Dunedin Cl BH22 23 G5
Dunedin Dr BH22 23 G5
Dunedin Gdns BH22 23 G5
Dunedin Gro BH23 45 G6
Dunford Cl BH25 47 F6
Dunford Rd BH12 54 C1
Dunkeld Rd BH3 40 A6
Dunlin Cl BH23 61 E2
Dunnock Cl BH22 23 G1
Dunstans La BH15 53 H1
Dunyeats Rd BH18 28 C6
Durdells Av BH11 31 F5
Durdells Gdns BH11 31 F6
Durland Cl BH25 49 B5
Durley Chine BH2 4 A6
Durley Chine Ct BH2 4 A6
Durley Chine Rd BH2 4 A4
Durley Chine Rd South BH2 4 A5
Durley Gdns BH2 4 B5
Durley Rd BH2 4 B5
Durley Rd South BH2 4 B5
Durlston Cres BH23 42 D2
Durlston Rd BH14 54 B4
Durnstown SO41 64 C5
Durrant Rd, Bournemouth BH2 4 C3
Durrant Rd, Poole BH14 54 B4
Durrant Way SO41 64 B5
Durrington Pl BH7 58 B1
Durrington Rd BH7 58 B1
Durweston Cl BH9 41 E1
Dymewood Rd BH21 8 A5

Eagle Rd BH12 55 F3
Earle Rd BH4 55 G5
Earles Rd BH21 8 B4
Earlham Dr BH14 54 B3
Earlsdon Way BH23 47 A7
Earlswood Pk BH25 48 E2
East Av, Bournemouth BH3 55 H1
East Av, New Milton BH25 47 E7
East Borough BH21 20 D3
East Cl BH25 47 F6
East Cliff Prom BH1 5 E5
East Cliff Way BH23 61 F1
East Ct BH14 54 B4
East Dorset Trade Pk BH21 23 E1
East Howe La BH10 31 H6
East La SO41 50 B5
East Overcliff Dr BH1 5 F5
East Quay Rd BH15 6 C5
East St, Poole BH15 6 C4
East St, Wimborne BH21 20 D4
East View Rd BH24 18 D5
East Way, Bournemouth BH8 41 E3
East Way, Wimborne BH21 27 F5
Eastcott Cl BH7 42 A6
Easter Rd BH9 40 D3
Eastern Way SO41 51 F3
Eastfield Ct BH24 19 E4
Eastfield La BH24 19 E3
Eastlake Av BH12 54 B1
Eastlands BH25 49 D5
Eastwood Av BH22 24 A2
Eastworth Rd BH31 7 A1
Eaton Rd BH13 55 F5
Ebblake Cl BH31 9 F1
Ebblake Ind Est BH31 7 F4
Ebenezer La BH24 18 C5
Ebor Cl BH22 24 B6
Ebor Rd BH12 38 C6
Eccles Rd BH15 52 B5
Eden Ct BH1 5 H4
Eden Gro BH21 21 E5
Edgarton Rd BH17 37 E1
Edgehill Rd BH9 40 B4
Edgemoor Rd BH22 14 D5
Edgon Cl BH22 23 G6
Edifred Rd BH9 32 D6
Edmondsham Ho BH2 4 C4
Edmondsham Rd BH31 7 B1
Edmunds Cl BH25 49 B6
Edward May Ct*, Mount Rd BH11 39 F1
Edward Rd, Bournemouth BH11 39 G2
Edward Rd, Christchurch BH23 44 C6
Edward Rd, Poole BH14 54 C2
Edwina Cl BH24 19 E2
Edwina Dr BH17 36 D2
Egdon Ct BH16 34 D3
Egdon Dr BH21 29 F2
Egerton Gdns BH8 41 F6
Egerton Rd BH8 41 F6
Egmont Cl BH24 16 D5
Egmont Dr BH24 16 D5
Egmont Gdns BH24 16 D5
Egmont Rd BH16 35 D6
Elderberry La BH23 60 C2
Eldon Av BH25 49 A6
Eldon Cl BH25 47 F7
Eldon Pl BH4 55 G3
Eldon Rd BH9 40 A3
Eleanor Dr BH11 30 C5
Eleanor Gdns BH23 43 E6
Elfin Dr BH22 23 H1
Elgar Rd BH10 31 H6
Elgin Rd, Bournemouth BH3 40 A6
Elgin Rd, Bournemouth BH3,4 56 A1
Elgin Rd, Poole BH14 54 A5
Elijah Cl BH15 52 A4
Elise Cl BH7 42 B6
Elizabeth Av BH23 43 F6
Elizabeth Cres SO41 50 C3
Elizabeth Ct BH1 5 G4
Elizabeth Gdns BH23 45 G6
Elizabeth Rd, Poole BH15 6 D2
Elizabeth Rd, Upton BH16 34 D2
Elizabeth Rd, Wimborne BH21 21 E3
Elkhams Cl SO41 50 A5
Ellesfield Dr BH22 24 A6
Ellingham Rd BH25 47 E7
Elliott Rd BH11 38 D2
Elm Av, Christchurch BH23 43 E4
Elm Av, New Milton BH25 49 B5
Elm Gdns BH4 55 G2
Elm Tree Walk BH22 32 B2
Elm Vw BH24 19 F6
Elmers Way BH23 64 C1
Elmes Rd BH9 40 B2
Elmgate Dr BH7 42 A6
Elmhurst Rd, Bournemouth BH11 31 F5
Elmhurst Rd, Ferndown BH22 14 C5
Elmhurst Way BH22 14 C5
Elmore Dr BH24 15 G1
Elms Av BH14 53 H6
Elms Cl BH14 54 A5
Elms Way BH6 59 E3
Elmstead Rd BH13 63 F1
Elmwood Way BH23 47 B7
Elphinstone Rd BH23 47 C6
Eltham Cl BH7 42 B6
Elvin Cl SO41 50 A1
Elwyn Rd BH1 57 E2
Elysium Ct BH22 24 B5
Embankment Way BH24 18 D6
Emberley Cl BH22 24 C2
Emerald Cl BH24 9 G6
Emerson Cl BH15 6 C4
Emerson Rd BH15 6 C4
Emily Cl BH23 43 F5
Encombe Cl BH12 39 E5
Endfield Cl BH23 43 F5
Endfield Rd, Bournemouth BH9 40 C3
Endfield Rd, Christchurch BH23 43 E5
Enfield Av BH15 37 G6
Enfield Cres BH15 53 G1
Enfield Rd BH15 37 F6
Englands Way BH11 38 D1
Ensbury Av BH10 39 H3
Ensbury Cl BH10 40 A3
Ensbury Ct BH10 40 A2
Ensbury Park Rd BH9 40 B3
Enterprise Pk BH31 7 F3
Enterprise Way BH23 33 F2
Erica Dr BH21 26 E4
Ericksen Rd BH11 39 G1
Erinbank Mansions BH1 57 E3
Erpingham Rd BH12 55 F2
Esmonde Way BH17 37 G5
Esplanade BH13 63 F2
Essex Av BH23 43 F4
Ethelbert Rd BH21 21 E5
Eton Gdns BH4 55 H2
Ettrick Rd BH13 55 F5
Eucalyptus Av BH24 16 A5
Euston Gro BH24 18 D5
Evans Cl, Bournemouth BH11 39 E3
Evans Cl, Ringwood BH24 15 G1
Evelyn Rd BH9 40 C3
Evening Glade BH22 24 B5
Eventide Homes BH8 41 H3
Everdene Cl BH22 23 H6
Everest Rd BH23 44 B6
Everglades Cl BH22 24 A1
Evergreen Cl BH21 8 B4
Evergreens BH24 15 H1
Evering Av BH12 38 B4
Evering Gdns BH12 38 C4
Everlea Cl SO41 50 A4
Everon Gdns BH25 49 C5
Evershot Rd BH8 41 G3
Everton Rd SO41 50 A1
Evesham Cl BH7 42 B5
Evesham Ct BH13 55 F5
Exbourne Manor BH1 57 E3
Exbury Dr BH11 31 E5
Excelsior Rd BH14 54 B4
Exeter Cres BH2 4 D5
Exeter Ct BH23 47 C8
Exeter Grange BH2 4 D5
Exeter La BH2 4 D4
Exeter Park Mansions BH2 4 D5
Exeter Park Rd BH2 4 D5
Exeter Rd BH2 4 D4
Exton Rd BH6 58 C1
Eynon Mews BH24 18 C5

Factory Rd BH16 34 E3
Fair Lea BH2 4 B6
Fairfield BH23 43 G6
Fairfield Cl, Christchurch BH23 43 G6
Fairfield Cl, Wimborne BH21 21 G3
Fairfield Rd, New Milton BH25 47 F7
Fairfield Rd, Wimborne BH21 21 E4
Fairhaven Ct BH5 57 H3
Fairies Dr BH22 24 B5
Fairlie BH24 19 E3
Fairlie Pk BH24 19 E2
Fairmile Par BH23 43 F4
Fairmile Rd BH23 43 E4
Fairthorn Ct BH2 4 D1
Fairview Cres BH18 28 C5
Fairview Dr BH18 28 C6
Fairview Pk BH14 54 B4
Fairview Rd BH18 28 C5
Fairway Dr BH23 59 F2
Fairway Rd BH14 54 C6
Fairways BH22 24 B2
Fairwood Rd BH31 7 F3
Falcon Dr BH23 61 E3
Falconer Dr BH15 52 A2
Falkland Sq BH15 6 C3
Fancy Rd BH12 38 A4
Farcroft Rd BH12 54 A1
Farm Cl BH24 18 C3
Farm Ct BH21 22 A4
Farm La BH23 60 D3
Farm La North BH25 49 B7
Farm La South BH25 49 B7
Farm Rd BH22 14 A4
Farmdene Cl BH23 45 G5
Farmers Walk, Lymington SO41 50 A5
Farmers Walk, Wimborne BH21 20 D2
Farnham Rd BH12 39 F6
Farriers Cl BH21 22 A2
Farwell Cl BH23 44 A3
Farwell Rd BH12 38 B2
Fawcett Rd BH25 49 A5
Fawley Grn BH8 41 F2
Fawn Gdns BH25 48 A3
Fayrewood Ct BH31 7 C1
Felton Cres BH23 47 A6
Felton Ct BH14 53 H1
Felton Rd BH14 53 G1
Fenleigh Cl BH25 49 C6
Fenton Rd BH6 58 C2
Fenwick Ct BH8 57 E2
Fern Bank, Bournemouth BH2 4 D3
Fern Bank, Wimborne BH21 8 A5
Fern Barrow BH12 39 G5
Fern Cl BH23 43 H4
Ferncroft Gdns BH10 32 A5
Ferncroft Rd BH10 32 A5
Ferndale Rd BH25 48 C2
Ferndown By-Pass BH21,22 22 B3
Ferndown Ind Est BH21 23 F1
Fernglade BH25 48 C3
Fernheath Cl BH11 39 F2
Fernheath Rd BH11 39 F2
Fernhill Cl BH17 38 A2
Fernhill Flats BH2 4 D3
Fernhill La BH25 48 B1
Fernhill Rd BH25 48 B3
Fernlea Av BH22 24 A4
Fernlea Cl, Ferndown BH22 24 A4
Fernlea Cl, Ringwood BH24 15 G2

Fernlea Gdns BH22 24 A4
Fernside Av BH14 53 G3
Fernside Pk BH21 23 F1
Fernside Rd, Bournemouth BH9 40 A4
Fernside Rd, Ferndown BH22 14 B5
Fernside Rd, Poole BH15 53 F2
Fernway Cl BH21 22 A4
Fernwood Cl BH24 16 B2
Ferris Av BH8 41 F2
Ferris Cl BH8 41 F2
Ferris Pl BH8 41 F2
Ferry Rd, Bournemouth BH6 59 F5
Ferry Rd, Poole BH15 6 A5
Ferry Way BH13 62 C6
Feversham Av BH8 41 G4
Field Mews BH21 21 F4
Field Pl, New Milton BH25 47 E7
Field Pl, Verwood BH31 7 B1
Field Way, Christchurch BH23 45 G5
Field Way, Wimborne BH21 26 F2
Fieldway BH24 18 D3
Finchfield Av BH11 31 E5
Fir Av BH25 49 C5
Fir Cl BH22 14 A3
Fir Tree Cl BH24 15 F4
Fir Tree La BH23 45 G4
Fir Vale Rd BH1 5 E3
Firbank Rd BH9 40 D5
Firmain Rd BH12 38 D3
Firmount Cl SO41 50 B5
Firs Glen Rd, Bournemouth BH9 40 A5
Firs Glen Rd, Ferndown BH22 14 B4
Firs Glen Rd, Verwood BH31 7 C3
Firs La BH14 62 C1
Firshill BH23 45 H5
Firside Rd BH21 27 E6
First Marine Av BH25 49 B8
Firsway BH16 34 E2
Firtree Cres SO41 50 A2
Fishermans Av BH6 58 B3
Fishermans Bank BH23 60 C3
Fishermans Rd BH15 6 C5
Fishermans Walk BH6 58 B4
Fitzharris Av BH9 40 C5
Fitzmaurice Rd BH23 43 E6
Fitzpain Cl BH22 23 H6
Fitzpain Rd BH22 23 H6
Fitzwilliam Cl BH11 30 D6
Fitzworth Av BH16 35 E6
Flaghead Chine BH13 63 F2
Flaghead Rd BH13 63 F2
Flambard Av BH23 43 F5
Flambard Rd BH14 54 B4
Flazen Cl BH11 38 C1
Fleets Corner BH17 36 D5
Fleets Est BH15 52 D1
Fleets La BH15 36 D6
Fleetsbridge Bsns Centre BH17 36 C6
Fleetwood Ct BH15 37 E6
Fletcher Cl BH10 39 H1
Fletcher Rd BH10 39 H1
Floral Farm BH21 29 H1
Florence Rd, Bournemouth BH5 57 H3
Florence Rd, Poole BH14 54 C3
Floriston Gdns BH25 48 E4
Flower Ct BH21 21 E5
Folly Farm La BH24 16 C1
Fontmell Rd BH18 36 D3
Footners La BH23 44 A4
Ford Cl BH22 24 C1
Ford La BH22 24 C1
Foreland Cl BH23 42 D1
Foreland Rd BH16 35 D6
Forest Cl BH23 45 G5
Forest Ct BH25 48 C4
Forest Edge Cl, Lymington SO41 64 B4
Forest Edge Cl, Ringwood BH24 15 G1
Forest Edge Dr BH24 9 G6
Forest Edge Rd BH24 19 G6
Forest Hills Ct BH24 19 F5
Forest Ho BH1 5 F5
Forest La, Ringwood BH24 19 G5
Forest La, Verwood BH31 7 A2
Forest Links Rd BH22 13 G5
Forest Oak Dr BH25 48 C2
Forest Pines BH25 48 C2
Forest Rd, Ferndown BH22 14 C3
Forest Rd, Poole BH13 55 F5
Forest Rise BH23 45 G4
Forest View Cl BH9 40 D2
Forest View Dr BH21 23 F2
Forest View Rd BH9 40 D2
Forest Vw BH25 46 F1
Forest Way, Christchurch BH23 45 G4
Forest Way, Lymington SO41 50 A4
Forest Way, Wimborne BH21 23 F3
Forestlake Av BH24 19 F5
Forestside Gdns BH24 19 E2
Forge La BH31 7 A3
Forsyth Gdns BH10 39 H3
Fort Cumberland Cl BH15 35 F7
Fortescue Rd, Bournemouth BH3 40 C6
Fortescue Rd, Poole BH12 38 C6
Forton Cl BH10 32 B6
Fountain Way BH23 59 H1
Four Wells Rd BH21 21 H1
Fox Fld SO41 50 B5
Fox La BH21 22 C4
Foxbury Rd BH24 15 H5
Foxcote Gdns BH25 48 A4
Foxcroft Dr BH21 22 A3
Foxes Cl BH31 7 C3
Foxglove Cl BH23 45 F5
Foxglove Pl BH25 48 E3
Foxgloves BH16 34 C2
Foxhills BH31 7 E2
Foxholes Rd, Bournemouth BH6 59 E4
Foxholes Rd, Poole BH15 37 H6
Foxwood Av BH23 60 C2
Frampton Cl BH25 48 D2
Frampton Pl BH24 18 C4
Frampton Rd BH9 40 D5
Frances Ct BH23 47 C7
Frances Rd BH1 5 H2
Francis Av BH11 38 C1
Francis Rd BH12 54 D2
Frankland Cres BH14 54 D4
Franklin Rd, Bournemouth BH9 40 D1
Franklin Rd, New Milton BH25 48 D3
Franklyn Cl BH16 34 D2
Franks Way BH12 38 A6
Frankston Rd BH6 58 C3
Fraser Ct*, Marryat Rd BH25 48 A4
Fraser Rd BH12 39 E4
Freda Rd BH23 59 F1
Frederica Rd BH9 40 B5
Freemans Cl BH21 22 B3
Freemans La BH21 22 A3
French Rd BH17 36 D3
Frenchs Farm Rd BH16 34 B3
Frensham Cl BH10 40 B1
Freshwater Dr BH15 35 F6
Freshwater Rd BH23 61 G1
Friars Rd BH23 61 E2
Friars Walk BH25 49 B6
Fritham Gdns BH8 41 F1
Frobisher Av BH12 39 E3
Frobisher Cl, Christchurch BH23 60 D2
Frobisher Cl, Ringwood BH24 19 F3
Frost Rd BH11 39 E1
Froud Way BH21 27 E6
Fryer Cl BH11 31 G5
Fryers Copse BH21 22 B3
Fryers Rd BH21 8 A4
Frys La SO41 50 A4
Fulmar Rd BH23 61 E3
Fulwood Av BH11 30 D5
Furnell Rd BH15 6 D5
Furze Cft BH25 49 B5
Furze Hill Dr BH14 54 B5
Furzebank La BH10 39 H3
Furzebrook Cl BH17 37 F2
Furzehill BH21 11 E6
Furzelands Rd BH21 8 B4
Furzey Rd BH16 34 D4
Furzy Whistlers Cl BH23 64 C1
Gainsborough Av BH25 48 C2
Gainsborough Ct BH5 58 B2
Gainsborough Rd, Bournemouth BH7 41 H6
Gainsborough Rd, Ringwood BH24 15 H2
Gallop Way BH12 39 H5
Galloway Rd BH15 35 F6
Gallows Dr BH22 32 A1
Galton Av BH23 59 F2
Garden Cl BH25 49 B5
Garden Court Cotts BH22 14 A3
Garden Ct BH1 57 G1
Garden Ho BH1 5 G4
Garden La BH24 15 H3
Garden Walk BH22 24 B1
Gardens Cres BH14 62 C1
Gardens Ct BH15 53 F4
Gardens Rd BH14 62 C1
Gardens Vw BH1 57 E2
Gardner Rd, Christchurch BH23 43 E6
Gardner Rd, Ringwood BH24 19 E5
Garfield Av BH1 57 F1
Garland Rd BH15 6 D1
Garsdale Cl BH11 31 F5
Garth Cl BH24 15 F2
Garth Rd BH9 40 C3
Gaydon Rise BH11 30 D6
Geneva Av BH6 58 D3
George Rd, Lymington SO41 51 D2
George Rd, Wimborne BH21 26 F3
Georges Mews BH21 26 F3
Georgian Cl BH24 18 D3
Georgian Way BH10 32 B6
Georgina Cl BH12 39 G5
Gerald Rd BH3 40 D6
Germaine Cl BH23 47 A7
Gervis Cres BH14 54 A2
Gervis Pl BH1 4 D4
Gervis Rd BH1 5 F4
Gibson Rd BH17 37 F5
Giddylake BH21 21 E2
Gilbert Rd BH8 41 F6
Gillam Rd BH10 32 A6
Gillett Rd BH12 39 H5
Gillingham Cl BH9 41 E1
Gillingham Rd SO41 51 E4
Gilpin Hill SO41 64 B5
Gilpin Pl SO41 64 B4
Gin Alley BH13 62 C5
Gipsy La BH24 18 D3
Gladdis Rd BH11 39 E1
Gladelands Cl BH18 36 A1
Gladelands Pk BH22 24 C1
Gladelands Way BH18 36 A1
Gladstone Cl BH23 60 B2
Gladstone Rd, Bournemouth BH7 57 H2
Gladstone Rd, Poole BH12 54 B2
Gladstone Rd West BH1 57 G2
Glamis Av BH10 32 A6
Gleadowe Av BH23 59 F1
Glebefields SO41 51 D3
Glen Cl BH25 47 E6
Glen Dr BH25 47 D7
Glen Fern Rd BH1 5 E3
Glen Rd, Bournemouth BH5 57 H3
Glen Rd, Poole BH14 54 A2
Glenair Av BH14 53 H3
Glenair Cres BH14 53 H3
Glenair Rd BH14 53 H3
Glenavon BH25 49 D5
Glenavon Rd BH23 47 A5
Glencoe Rd, Bournemouth BH7 41 H6
Glencoe Rd, Poole BH12 54 C1
Glendale Av BH22 24 A2
Glendale Cl, Christchurch BH23 42 D3
Glendale Cl, Wimborne BH21 21 E3
Glendale Ct BH23 42 D3
Glendale Rd BH6 59 G4
Glendales BH25 47 E6
Glendene Pk BH25 46 F1
Glendon Av BH10 31 H4
Gleneagles Av BH14 54 C4
Gleneagles Cl BH22 24 C2
Glenferness Av BH3 40 A6
Glengariff Rd BH14 54 C4
Glengarry BH25 49 D5
Glengarry Way BH23 61 F2
Glenives Cl BH24 16 A3
Glenmeadows Dr BH10 31 G6
Glenmoor Cl BH10 40 A3
Glenmoor Rd, Bournemouth BH9 40 A4
Glenmoor Rd, Ferndown BH22 23 H5
Glenmount Dr BH14 54 A2
Glenroyd Gdns BH6 59 E3
Glenside BH25 47 D7
Glenville Cl BH23 47 C5
Glenville Gdns BH10 39 H2
Glenville Rd, Bournemouth BH10 39 H2
Glenville Rd, Christchurch BH23 47 C5
Glenwood Cl BH22 14 A4
Glenwood La BH22 14 B4
Glenwood Rd, Ferndown BH22 14 A4
Glenwood Rd, Verwood BH31 7 B3
Glenwood Way BH22 14 A4
Glissons BH22 23 F6
Globe La BH15 6 C4
Gloucester Rd, Bournemouth BH7 57 H1
Gloucester Rd, Poole BH12 54 D1
Glynville Cl BH21 21 H1
Glynville Ct BH21 21 H1
Glynville Rd BH21 21 H1
Goathorn Cl BH16 35 F5
Godmanston Cl BH17 37 H3
Gods Blessing La BH21 11 G3
Godshill Cl BH8 41 F2
Golden Cres SO41 50 A5
Goldenleas Dr BH11 38 C1
Goldfinch Cl BH25 49 A5
Goldfinch Rd BH17 36 A4
Golf Links Rd, Broadstone BH18 28 C6
Golf Links Rd, Ferndown BH22 24 B3
Goliath Rd BH15 35 F7
Good Rd BH12 38 B6
Gooseberry La BH24 18 C5
Gordon Ct BH4 55 H3
Gordon Mount BH23 47 C6
Gordon Rd, Bournemouth BH1 57 F2
Gordon Rd, Christchurch BH23 47 C6
Gordon Rd, Poole BH12 55 F2
Gordon Rd, Wimborne BH21 21 F4
Gordon Rd South BH12 55 F2
Gordon Way BH23 44 A4
Gore Grange BH25 49 A5
Gore Rd BH25 47 E5
Gore Rd Ind Est BH25 48 A4
Gorey Rd BH12 38 C3
Gorleston Rd BH12 55 E2
Gorley Rd BH24 19 E1
Gorse Cl, New Milton BH25 48 E3
Gorse Cl, Ringwood BH24 15 F2
Gorse Hill Cl BH15 53 G2
Gorse Hill Cres BH15 53 G2
Gorse Hill Rd BH15 53 G1
Gorse Knoll Dr BH31 7 B1
Gorse La BH16 34 E2
Gorse Rd BH21 27 E5
Gorsecliff Ct BH5 57 F3
Gorsecliff Rd BH10 40 A3
Gorsefield Rd BH25 48 D2
Gorseland Ct BH22 24 A6
Gort Rd, Bournemouth BH11 39 G1
Gort Rd, Poole BH17 36 C3
Gosling Cl BH17 37 G5
Gough Cres BH17 36 C3
Grafton Cl, Bournemouth BH3 40 C6
Grafton Cl, Christchurch BH23 60 B2
Grafton Rd BH3 40 C6
Grammar School La BH21 20 D4
Granby Rd BH9 32 D6
Grand Av BH6 58 C3
Grange BH21 10 D5
Grange Cl SO41 50 B5
Grange Ct BH1 5 H3
Grange Gdns BH12 38 D5
Grange Rd, Bournemouth BH6 58 D4
Grange Rd, Broadstone BH18 36 C1
Grange Rd, Christchurch BH23 45 E6
Grange Rd, Ringwood BH24 15 G4
Grange Rd Bsns Centre BH23 45 E6
Grantham Rd BH1 57 G1
Grantley Rd BH7 57 H2
Grants Av BH1 57 G1
Grants Cl BH1 41 G6
Granville Pl BH1 4 D3
Granville Rd, Bournemouth BH5 58 A3
Granville Rd, Poole BH12 54 A2
Grasmere Cl BH23 42 D2
Grasmere Gdns BH25 48 C2
Grasmere Rd, Bournemouth BH5 58 A4
Grasmere Rd, Poole BH13 62 C5
Gravel Hill, Poole BH17 37 E3
Gravel Hill, Wimborne BH21 29 E2
Gravel La BH24 18 C3,4
Gray Cl BH17 37 G5
Graycot Cl BH10 31 H5
Grays Yd BH15 6 B5
Grayson Ct BH22 24 A5
Greaves Cl BH10 39 H2
Grebe Cl, Christchurch BH23 60 D2
Grebe Cl, Lymington SO41 51 E4
Grebe Cl, Poole BH17 36 A5
Green Acre BH25 49 B7
Green Acres BH23 60 D1
Green Acres Cl BH24 16 D2
Green Bottom BH21 21 H1
Green Cl BH15 6 C4
Green Gdns BH15 6 D5
Green La, Bournemouth BH10 39 H2
Green La, Christchurch BH23 46 C2
Green La, Ferndown BH22 31 F1
Green La, New Milton BH25 49 C6
Green La, Ringwood BH24 18 D4
Green Pk BH1 57 F3
Green Rd, Bournemouth BH9 40 C4
Green Rd, Poole BH15 6 C4
Greenacre Cl BH16 34 D4
Greenacres BH13 55 F4
Greenacres Cl BH10 32 A4
Greenbanks Cl SO41 51 E3
Greenclose La BH21 21 F4
Greenfield Gdns BH25 49 C6
Greenfield Rd BH15 37 G6
Greenfinch Cl BH17 36 B3
Greenfinch Walk BH24 19 E6
Greenhayes BH18 36 D3
Greenhays Rise BH21 21 E3
Greenhill Cl BH21 21 F2
Greenhill La BH21 21 F2
Greenhill Rd BH21 21 F2
Greenmead Av SO41 50 A4
Greenside Ct BH25 49 C8
Greensleeves Av BH18 28 D5
Greensome Dr BH22 24 B2
Greenway Cres BH16 34 B3
Greenways, Christchurch BH23 47 A6
Greenways, Lymington SO41 51 D2
Greenways Av BH8 41 E2
Greenways Ct BH22 24 B5
Greenwood Av, Ferndown BH22 24 A2
Greenwood Av, Poole BH14 54 B6
Greenwood Copse BH24 16 A3
Greenwood Rd BH9 40 A4
Greenwood Way BH24 16 A3
Greenwoods BH25 49 C5
Grenfell Rd BH9 40 C1
Grenville Cl BH24 19 F3
Grenville Ct, Bournemouth BH4 4 A2

Grenville Ct,
Poole BH15 6 C4
Grenville Rd BH21 21 E4
Gresham Rd BH9 40 D4
Greycot Cl BH21 8 A4
Greystoke Av BH11 31 E5
Griffin Ct BH21 21 E5
Griffiths Gdns BH10 31 G6
Grosvener Ct BH1 5 H4
Grosvenor Cl BH24 15 F1
Grosvenor Ct BH1 57 F3
Grosvenor Gdns BH1 57 G2
Grosvenor Rd BH4 55 G4
Grove Mansions BH1 5 H4
Grove Rd,
Bournemouth BH1 5 F4
Grove Rd,
New Milton BH25 49 B8
Grove Rd, Poole BH12 54 A1
Grove Rd,
Wimborne BH21 21 E4
Grove Rd East BH23 43 F6
Grove Rd West BH23 43 F6
Groveley Rd,
Bournemouth BH4 55 G4
Groveley Rd,
Christchurch BH23 60 B1
Grovely Av BH5 57 H3
Grower Gdns BH11 39 F1
Guernsey Rd BH12 38 C3
Guest Av BH12 55 E1
Guest Cl BH12 55 F1
Guest Rd BH16 34 D3
Guildford Ct BH4 55 H3
Guildhall Ct BH15 6 B4
Guildhall Ct*,
New Orch BH15 52 D5
Guildhill Rd BH6 59 E4
Gulliver Cl BH14 62 D1
Gullivers Ct BH21 20 D3
Gundrymoor Trading Est BH21 14 B1
Gunville Cres BH9 41 E1
Gurjun Cl BH16 34 C2
Gurney Rd BH21 28 A4
Gussage Rd BH12 39 E5
Guys Cl BH24 18 D5
Gwenlyn Rd BH16 34 D3
Gwynne Rd BH12 54 D1

Haarlem Mews BH23 60 A1
Hadden Rd BH8 41 F4
Haddons Dr BH21 8 A5
Hadley Way BH18 36 A1
Hadow Rd BH10 39 G2
Hadrian Cl BH22 32 A1
Hadrian Way BH21 28 A3
Hahnemann Rd BH2 4 B5
Haig Av BH13 54 D5
Hainault Dr BH31 7 C2
Haking Rd BH23 44 B6
Hale Av BH25 49 C5
Hale Gdns BH25 49 C5
Halewood Way BH23 43 F6
Halifax Way BH23 61 E1
Hall Rd BH11 39 E1
Halstock Cres BH17 37 E3
Halter Path BH15 52 A4
Halter Rise BH21 22 B2
Halton Cl BH23 64 C2
Ham La,
Wimborne BH21 22 B4
Ham La,
Wimborne BH21 22 C3
Hamble Rd BH15 37 H6
Hambledon Gdns BH6 58 C2
Hambledon La BH6 58 B2
Hambledon Rd BH6,7 58 B1
Hamblin Way BH8 41 G2
Hamilton Cl,
Bournemouth BH1 57 F2
Hamilton Cl,
Christchurch BH23 60 C3
Hamilton Cl,
Poole BH15 52 A4
Hamilton Cres BH15 52 A4
Hamilton Ct,
Bournemouth BH8 5 H1
Hamilton Ct,
Lymington SO41 51 C3
Hamilton Rd,
Bournemouth BH1 57 F2
Hamilton Rd,
Poole BH15 52 A4
Hamilton Rd,
Wimborne BH21 28 A5
Hamilton Way BH25 49 A5
Hampden La BH6 58 B2
Hampreston Rd BH22 23 F6
Hampshire Cl BH23 43 F4
Hampshire Ct BH2 4 D3
Hampshire Ho BH2 4 D3
Hampton Dr BH24 18 D3
Handley Ct BH24 18 B5
Hanham Rd,
Corfe Mullen BH21 27 F5
Hanham Rd,
Wimborne BH21 20 D3
Hankinson Rd BH9 40 C5
Hanlon Cl BH11 39 F1
Hannington Rd BH7 58 A2
Hanover Grn BH17 37 G5
Harbeck Rd BH8 41 F1
Harbour Cl BH13 63 E3
Harbour Cres BH23 60 C2
Harbour Ct,
New Milton BH25 47 F8
Harbour Ct,
Poole BH13 63 E2
Harbour Hill Cres BH15 53 F2
Harbour Hill Rd BH15 53 F2
Harbour Lights BH15 53 G3
Harbour Rd BH6 59 G5
Harbour View Cl BH14 53 H2
Harbour View Ct*,
Princess Av BH23 59 H2
Harbour View Rd BH14 53 H2
Harbour Watch BH14 62 D2
Harcombe Cl BH17 37 F2
Harcourt Mews BH5 58 A3
Harcourt Rd BH5 58 A3
Hardy Cl,
Christchurch BH23 60 D2
Hardy Cl,
Ferndown BH22 14 B5
Hardy Cl,
New Milton BH25 48 A4
Hardy Cres BH21 21 F5
Hardy Rd,
Ferndown BH22 14 C5
Hardy Rd, Poole BH14 54 C2
Hare La,
Lymington SO41 48 F3
Hare La,
New Milton BH25 48 F4
Hares Grn BH7 42 A6
Harewood Av BH7 41 H5
Harewood Cres BH7 41 H5
Harewood Gdns BH7 41 H5
Harewood Pl BH7 58 B1
Harford Rd BH12 38 B5
Harkwood Dr BH15 52 A3
Harland Rd BH6 59 F4
Harness Cl BH21 22 A2
Harrier Dr BH21 29 F1
Harriers Cl BH23 45 G5
Harrington Ct BH23 47 A8
Harris Way BH25 48 D1
Harrison Av BH1 41 G6
Harrison Cl BH23 43 H3
Harrison Way BH22 14 B3
Harry Barrows Cl BH24 18 C5
Hart Cl BH25 48 A3
Harting Rd BH6 58 D1
Hartnell Ct BH21 27 E5
Harts La BH21 11 H2
Harts Way SO41 50 A4
Hartsbourne Dr BH7 42 B6
Harvey Rd,
Bournemouth BH5 58 A3
Harvey Rd,
Wimborne BH21 29 G2,3
Harwell Rd BH17 37 E5
Harwood Ct BH25 48 A4
Haskells Rd BH12 38 A6
Haslemere Av BH23 47 A6
Haslemere Pl BH23 47 B6
Hasler Rd BH17 37 E3
Haslop Rd BH21 21 H1
Hastings Rd,
Bournemouth BH8 41 H3
Hastings Rd,
Poole BH17 36 C3
Hatch Pond Rd BH17 37 E4
Hatfield Ct BH25 48 A3
Hatfield Gdns BH7 42 B5
Hathaway Rd BH6 58 D4
Hatherden Av BH14 53 H2
Havelock Rd BH12 55 F2
Havelock Way BH23 45 G4
Haven Ct SO41 51 C3
Haven Gdns BH25 49 C5
Haven Rd, Poole BH13 63 E3
Haven Rd,
Wimborne BH21 26 E4
Haverstock Rd BH9 40 D2
Haviland Mews*,
Haviland Rd BH7 57 H2
Haviland Rd,
Bournemouth BH7 57 H2
Haviland Rd,
Wimborne BH21 23 F1
Haviland Rd East BH7 57 H2
Haviland Rd West*,
Ashley Rd BH7 57 H2
Hawden Rd BH11 39 F3
Hawk Cl BH21 22 A1
Hawkchurch Gdns
BH17 37 G2
Hawker Cl BH21 29 G1
Hawkins Cl,
Christchurch BH23 60 D2
Hawkins Cl,
Ringwood BH24 19 E3
Hawkins Rd BH12 39 E3
Hawkwood Rd BH5 57 H2
Haworth Cl BH23 43 G4
Hawthorn Cl BH25 48 D3
Hawthorn Dr,
Lymington SO41 64 B5
Hawthorn Dr,
Poole BH17 36 A3
Hawthorn Rd,
Bournemouth BH9 40 B4
Hawthorn Rd,
Christchurch BH23 44 B5
Haydon Rd BH13 55 F5
Hayes Av BH7 41 G6
Hayes Cl BH21 22 A4
Hayes La BH21 22 A4
Hayeswood Rd BH21 21 H3
Haymoor Rd BH15 37 H5
Haynes Av BH15 53 E2
Haysoms Cl BH25 49 C6
Hayward Cres BH31 7 B3
Hayward Way BH31 7 A3
Haywards Farm Cl BH31 7 A3
Haywards La BH21 26 E3
Hazel Cl BH23 45 G4
Hazel Ct*,
Station Rd BH25 49 C5
Hazel Dr BH22 23 H1
Hazeldene BH18 36 C1
Hazell Av BH10 39 G3
Hazelton Cl BH7 42 A6
Hazelwood Av BH25 48 A3
Hazelwood Dr BH31 7 E4
Hazlebury Rd BH17 36 C6
Hazlemere Dr BH24 15 H3
Headlands Bsns Pk BH24 18 C2
Heads Farm Cl BH10 32 B6
Heads La BH10 32 B6
Headswell Av BH10 32 B6
Headswell Cres BH10 32 B6
Headswell Gdns BH10 32 B6
Heanor Cl BH10 39 H2
Heath Av BH15 37 E6
Heath Cl BH21 22 A1
Heath Farm Cl BH22 23 H5
Heath Farm Rd BH22 23 H5
Heath Farm Way BH22 23 H5
Heath Rd,
Christchurch BH23 47 C6
Heath Rd,
Lymington SO41 50 A2
Heath Rd,
Ringwood BH24 15 F2
Heath Rd West BH23 25 G3
Heathcote Rd BH5 57 H2
Heather Bank Rd BH4 55 G3
Heather Cl,
Bournemouth BH8 41 F1
Heather Cl,
Christchurch BH23 47 C5
Heather Cl,
Lymington SO41 50 B2
Heather Cl,
Ringwood BH24 15 G3
Heather Cl,
Wimborne BH21 28 A5
Heather Ct BH22 14 D5
Heather Dr BH22 24 A1
Heather Rd BH10 39 H2
Heather View Rd BH12 39 E6
Heather Way BH22 24 A1
Heatherbrae La BH16 34 D4
Heatherdell BH16 34 C3
Heatherdown Rd BH22 14 C5
Heatherdown Way
BH22 14 D5
Heatherlands Rise
BH12 54 C1
Heatherlea Rd BH6 58 D4
Heathfield Av BH12 39 F4
Heathfield Rd BH22 14 C6
Heathfield Way BH22 14 C5
Heathlands Av BH22 32 A1
Heathlands Cl,
Christchurch BH23 44 A3
Heathlands Cl,
Verwood BH31 7 D2
Heathwood Av BH25 47 F6
Heathwood Rd BH9 40 A5
Heathy Cl BH25 49 A7
Heaton Rd BH10 39 G2
Heavytree Rd BH14 54 A3
Heckford La BH15 6 D1
Heckford Rd,
Poole BH15 6 D1
Heckford Rd,
Wimborne BH21 27 E5
Hedgerley BH25 49 C7
Heights Rd BH16 34 D2
Helic Ho BH21 20 D3
Helyar Rd BH8 41 H2
Henbest Cl BH21 22 B3
Henbury Cl,
Poole BH17 37 H3
Henbury Cl,
Wimborne BH21 26 F4
Henbury Rise BH21 26 F4
Henbury View Rd BH21 26 E4
Henchard Cl BH22 23 H6
Hendford Gdns BH10 40 A2
Hendford Rd BH10 40 A2
Hengist Rd BH1 57 F2
Hengistbury Rd,
Bournemouth BH6 59 F4
Hengistbury Rd,
New Milton BH25 47 F7
Henley Gdns BH7 42 A6
Hennings Park Rd
BH15 53 F1
Henville Rd BH8 57 E1
Herbert Av BH12 38 B4
Herbert Ct BH12 38 C5
Herbert Rd,
Bournemouth BH4 55 G5
Herbert Rd,
New Milton BH25 48 C4
Herberton Rd BH6 58 C2
Hercules Rd BH15 35 F7
Heritage Ct BH13 63 G1
Herm Rd BH12 38 C4
Hermitage Cl BH21 8 A4
Hermitage Rd BH14 53 H1
Heron Cl SO41 64 B5
Heron Court Rd BH3,9 40 D6
Heron Dr BH21 21 H1
Herstone Cl BH17 37 G3
Hertford Ct BH23 47 C7
Hesketh Cl BH24 16 A2
Hestan Cl BH23 42 D1
Heston Way BH22 14 A3
Hewitt Rd BH15 52 A3
Heysham Rd BH18 36 C1
Heytesbury Rd BH6 58 D2
Hibberd Way BH10 40 A3
Hibbs Cl BH16 34 E2
Hickes Cl BH11 30 D6
Hickory Cl BH16 34 C2
High Howe Cl BH11 38 D1
High Howe Gdns BH11 38 D1
High Howe La BH11 30 D6
High Mead BH22 23 F6
High Mead La BH22 31 E1
High Oaks Gdns BH11 30 D6
High Park Rd BH18 28 A6
High Ridge Cres BH25 48 D4
High St,
Ashley Heath BH24 9 H6
High St,
Christchurch BH23 59 H1
High St,
Lymington SO41 51 E3
High St, Poole BH15 6 B5
High St,
Ringwood BH24 18 B5
High St,
Wimborne BH21 20 D4
High St North BH15 6 D3
High Trees BH13 63 G1
High Trees Walk BH22 24 A1
High Way BH18 36 B1
Highbridge Rd BH14 54 B4
Highbury Cl BH25 48 C4
Highcliffe Rd BH23 45 E6
Higher Blandford Rd
BH18,21 28 A4
Higher Merley La BH21 28 A2
Highfield Av BH24 18 C3
Highfield Cl,
Lymington SO41 64 B5
Highfield Cl,
Wimborne BH21 28 A5
Highfield Dr BH24 18 C3
Highfield Gdns SO41 64 B5
Highfield Rd,
Bournemouth BH9 40 B3
Highfield Rd,
Ferndown BH22 14 A2
Highfield Rd,
Ringwood BH24 18 D4
Highfield Rd,
Wimborne BH21 28 A5
Highland Av BH23 47 C6
Highland Rd,
Poole BH14 54 A2
Highland Rd,
Wimborne BH21 21 F3
Highland View Cl BH21 21 F3
Highlands Cres BH10 31 G6
Highlands Rd BH25 49 B7
Highmoor Cl,
Poole BH14 54 B3
Highmoor Cl,
Wimborne BH21 27 F5
Highmoor Rd,
Bournemouth BH11 39 F3
Highmoor Rd,
Poole BH14 54 B4
Highmoor Rd,
Wimborne BH21 27 F5
Hightown Gdns BH24 19 E5
Hightown Hill BH24 19 F5
Hightown Ind Est BH24 18 D6
Hightown Rd BH24 18 C5
Hightrees Av BH8 41 H4
Highview Cl BH23 43 E2
Highview Gdns BH12 38 B6
Highwood La BH24 19 F1
Highwood Rd BH14 54 D2
Hilary Rd BH17 36 D3
Hilda Rd BH12 38 D6
Hiley Rd BH15 53 E1
Hill Cl BH23 64 B3
Hill La,
Bransgore BH23 64 B3
Hill La,
Christchurch BH23 44 C3
Hill St BH15 6 B4
Hill Ter BH21 21 H6
Hill View Ct BH21 27 E6
Hill View Rd BH22 23 G2
Hill Way BH24 15 H1
Hillary Rd BH23 44 B6
Hillbourne Rd BH17 36 C2
Hillbrow Rd BH6 58 B2
Hillcrest Av BH22 23 H1
Hillcrest Cl BH9 40 C1
Hillcrest Rd,
Bournemouth BH9 40 C1
Hillcrest Rd,
Poole BH12 54 A1
Hillcrest Rd,
Wimborne BH21 27 E5
Hillman Rd BH14 54 C2
Hillmeadow BH31 7 D4
Hillside Dr BH23 42 D2
Hillside Gdns BH21 27 E6
Hillside Mews BH21 27 E6
Hillside Rd, Poole BH12 39 E4
Hillside Rd,
Verwood BH31 7 C1
Hillside Rd,
Wimborne BH21 26 E4
Hillside Way BH21 27 E6
Hilltop Cl BH22 23 G1
Hilltop Rd,
Ferndown BH22 23 G1
Hilltop Rd,
Wimborne BH21 27 F5
Hillview Rd BH10 40 A1
Hiltom Rd BH24 18 D5
Hilton Cl BH15 53 H1
Hilton Rd BH25 48 D3
Hinchcliffe Cl BH15 52 B5
Hinchcliffe Rd BH15 52 A5
Hinton Rd BH1 5 E4
Hinton Wood BH1 5 F4
Hinton Wood Av BH23 45 H3
Hinton Wood La BH23 45 H3
Hive Gdns BH13 63 E3
Hobart Rd BH25 49 B5
Hobbs Pk BH24 15 H3
Hobbs Rd BH12 38 B4
Hobson Mansions BH1 5 G4
Hoburne Gdns BH23 45 F5
Hoburne La BH23 45 F6
Hodges Cl BH17 37 G5
Hogarth Way BH8 42 A4
Hogue Av BH10 32 A5
Holbury Cl BH8 41 G2
Holcombe Rd BH16 34 D3
Holdenhurst Av BH7 42 C6
Holdenhurst Rd BH8 5 G3
Holes Bay Rd BH15 6 A1
Holes Cl SO41 50 A1

Holland Way BH18 28 A5
Hollands Wood Dr BH25 48 C2
Hollies Cl SO41 64 B6
Holloway Av BH11 31 E5
Holly Cl, Ferndown BH22 14 A4
Holly Cl, Poole BH16 34 B3
Holly Cl, Ringwood BH24 15 G2
Holly Ct BH15 6 D1
Holly Gdns, Christchurch BH23 44 B4
Holly Gdns, Lymington SO41 51 C3
Holly Green Rise BH11 30 D6
Holly Gro BH31 7 A3
Holly Hedge La BH17 37 E4
Holly La, Christchurch BH23 47 D5
Holly La, New Milton BH25 48 E3
Holly Lodge BH13 55 F3
Holm Cl BH24 19 E2
Holm Oak Cl BH31 7 B1
Holme Rd BH23 47 C6
Holmfield Av BH7 42 C6
Holmhurst Av BH23 47 A6
Holmwood Garth BH24 19 F5
Holnest Rd BH17 37 E4
Holt La BH21 11 H2
Holt Rd, Poole BH12 55 E1
Holt Rd, Three Legged Cross BH21 8 A5
Holt Rd, Wimborne BH21 12 A1
Holworth Cl BH11 38 D1
Holyrood Cl BH17 36 C5
Holywell Cl BH17 37 F2
Home Farm Rd BH31 7 B2
Home Farm Way BH31 7 B2
Home Rd BH11 31 G5
Homedale Ho BH2 56 C1
Homedene Ho BH15 6 D3
Homegrange Ho SO41 51 D4
Homelands BH23 59 F1
Homelands Ho BH22 24 A3
Homeoaks Ho BH2 56 C1
Homeside Rd BH9 40 D3
Homeview Ho BH15 6 D3
Homewood Cl BH25 48 D4
Honeybourne Cres BH6 59 G3
Honeysuckle Gdns SO41 50 A5
Honeysuckle La BH17 36 B4
Honeysuckle Way BH23 45 E6
Honeywood Ho BH14 62 D2
Hood Cl BH10 39 G3
Hood Cres BH10 39 F3
Hooke Cl BH17 37 H3
Hop Cl BH16 34 B3
Hopkins Cl BH8 42 A3
Horace Rd BH5 57 G3
Hordle La SO41 50 B3
Hornbeam Way BH21 21 F3
Horning Rd BH12 55 E2
Horsa Cl BH6 59 E3
Horsa Ct BH6 59 E3
Horsa Rd BH6 59 E4
Horseshoe Cl BH21 22 A2
Horseshoe Ct BH1 5 E2
Horsham Av BH10 31 H5
Horton Cl BH9 41 E1
Horton Rd, Ringwood BH24 9 F6
Horton Rd, Wimborne BH21 8 A4
Horton Way BH31 7 A3
Hosiers La BH15 6 B5
Hosker Rd BH5 58 B3
Houlton Rd BH15 53 F3
Hounds Way BH21 22 A4
Hounslow Cl BH15 52 A5
Howard Cl BH23 60 D2
Howard Rd, Bournemouth BH8 41 E6
Howard Rd, Verwood BH31 7 B2
Howe Cl, Christchurch BH23 60 D2
Howe Cl, New Milton BH25 48 A4
Howe La BH31 7 B3
Howell Ho BH21 21 G1
Howeth Cl BH10 39 H1
Howeth Rd BH10 31 H6
Howton Cl BH10 31 H5
Howton Rd BH10 31 H5
Hoxley Rd BH10 32 A6
Hoyal Rd BH15 35 F6
Hudson Cl, Poole BH12 38 B3
Hudson Cl, Ringwood BH24 19 F3
Hughes Bsns Centre BH23 60 D1
Hull Cres BH11 30 D6
Hull Rd BH11 30 D6
Hull Way BH11 30 D6
Humber Rd BH22 24 D2
Hungerfield Cl BH23 64 B2
Hungerford Rd BH8 41 F2
Hunt Rd, Christchurch BH23 44 C6
Hunt Rd, Poole BH15 53 G2
Hunter Cl, Christchurch BH23 61 E1
Hunter Cl, Wimborne BH21 22 B2
Hunters Cl BH31 7 F3
Huntfield Rd BH9 40 D2
Huntick Rd BH16 34 A1
Huntingdon Dr BH21 29 F2
Huntingdon Gdns BH23 43 F3
Huntly Rd BH3 39 H6
Huntvale Rd BH9 40 D2
Hurdles Mead SO41 51 E4
Hurn Cl BH24 16 D1
Hurn Court La BH23 33 H4
Hurn La BH24 16 D1
Hurn Rd, Christchurch BH23 42 C1
Hurn Rd, Ringwood BH24 16 C6
Hurn Way BH23 42 D5
Hursley Cl BH7 42 C6
Hurst Cl, Christchurch BH23 47 D5
Hurst Cl, New Milton BH25 47 E7
Hurst Ct, Christchurch BH23 47 B7
Hurst Ct, Lymington SO41 51 C3
Hurst Hill BH14 54 B6
Hurst Rd, Lymington SO41 51 E4
Hurst Rd, Ringwood BH24 18 C3
Hurstbourne Av BH23 45 H4
Hurstdene Rd BH8 41 F2
Hussar Cl BH23 43 E6
Hyacinth Cl BH17 36 A4
Hyde Cl SO41 64 C5
Hyde Rd BH10 31 G5
Hynesbury Rd BH23 61 F1
Hythe Rd BH15 37 H6

Ibbertson Cl BH8 42 A4
Ibbertson Rd BH8 41 H3
Ibbertson Way BH8 42 A4
Ibbett Rd BH10 39 G2
Ibsley Cl BH8 41 F6
Iddesleigh Rd BH3 40 C6
Iford Cl BH6 59 E2
Iford Gdns BH7 42 C6
Iford La BH6 42 D6
Imber Dr BH23 47 B7
Imbre Ct BH13 63 F2
Inglegreen Cl BH25 49 A6
Inglesham Way BH15 52 A3
Inglewood Av BH8 41 H3
Inglewood Dr BH25 49 D5
Ingram Walk BH21 21 E4
Ingworth Rd BH12 55 F1
Insley Cres BH18 28 A5
Inveravon BH23 60 D3
Inverclyde Ho BH14 54 B3
Inverclyde Rd BH14 54 B3
Inverleigh Rd BH6 58 C2
Inverness Rd BH13 63 E2
Ipswich Rd BH4 55 G2
Iris Rd BH9 40 B4
Irvine Way BH23 44 B6
Irving La BH6 58 D3
Irving Rd BH6 58 C3
Isaacs Cl BH12 39 G5
Island View Av BH23 61 E2
Island View Cl SO41 51 E4
Island View Ct BH25 49 B7
Island View Rd BH25 47 D7
Ivamy Pl BH11 39 E3
Ivor Rd, Poole BH15 52 C5
Ivor Rd, Wimborne BH21 27 F6
Ivy Cl BH24 15 G3
Ivy Rd BH21 29 E2
Iwerne Cl BH9 32 D6

Jacklin Ct BH18 28 C6
Jackson Gdns BH12 38 B6
Jackson Rd BH12 54 C1
Jacmar Ct*, Ashley Rd BH25 48 C4
Jacobean Cl BH23 47 C6
Jacobs Rd BH15 35 F7
Jacqueline Rd BH12 38 B5
James Rd BH12 55 F2
Jameson Rd BH9 40 B4
Janred Ct BH25 47 F8
Jaundrells Cl BH25 48 D4
Jays Ct BH23 47 C7
Jefferson Av BH1 57 G1
Jellicoe Cl BH14 53 G2
Jellicoe Dr BH23 60 D2
Jenner Cl BH31 7 B1
Jennings Rd BH14 54 B4
Jephcote Rd BH11 39 E1
Jersey Cl BH12 38 C3
Jersey Rd BH12 38 C3
Jesmond Av BH23 47 A7
Jessica Av BH31 7 A2
Jessopp Cl BH10 32 C6
Jessopp Rd BH21 22 A3
Jewell Rd BH8 42 A4
Jimmy Brown Av BH22 14 B1
Johnson Rd BH21 23 F1
Johnston Rd BH15 37 F6
Johnstone Rd BH23 60 B2
Jolliffe Av BH15 53 F3
Jolliffe Rd BH15 6 D1
Jordans La SO41 64 C4
Joshua Cl BH15 35 F7
Jowitt Dr BH25 49 A5
Joyce Dickson Cl BH24 19 E5
Joys Rd BH21 8 A4
Jubilee Cl, Ringwood BH24 19 E4
Jubilee Cl, Wimborne BH21 28 A4
Jubilee Cres BH12 54 C2
Jubilee Ct SO41 64 B6
Jubilee Gdns BH10 39 H3
Jubilee Rd, Poole BH12 54 C2
Jubilee Rd, Wimborne BH21 28 A4
Julia Cl BH23 47 A7
Julians Rd BH21 20 C4
Julyan Av BH12 39 F4
Jumpers Av BH23 43 E5
Jumpers Rd BH23 43 E6
Junction Rd, Bournemouth BH9 40 C5
Junction Rd, Poole BH16 35 E6
Juniper Cl, Ferndown BH22 13 H6
Juniper Cl, Wimborne BH21 8 B4
Jupiter Way BH21 28 A3
Justin Gdns BH10 32 B6

Kangaw Pl BH15 35 F8
Kate Ct, Poole BH15 6 C4
Kate Ct, Ringwood BH24 18 D3
Katherine Chance Cl BH23 44 A3
Katterns Cl BH23 43 E3
Kay Cl BH23 60 C1
Keats Av SO41 51 D3
Keeble Cl BH10 32 A5
Keeble Cres BH10 32 A4
Keeble Rd BH10 32 A5
Keepers La BH21 23 E3
Keighley Av BH18 36 B2
Keith Rd BH3 39 H6
Kellaway Rd BH17 37 G4
Kelly Cl BH17 37 G5
Kelsall Gdns BH25 48 B4
Kemp Rd BH9 40 B5
Ken Rd BH6 59 E4
Kenilworth Cl BH25 48 C4
Kenilworth Ct BH13 63 G1
Kenilworth Ct*, Stour Rd BH23 59 G1
Kennard Ct BH25 48 B4
Kennard Rd BH25 48 A3
Kennart Rd BH17 36 C6
Kenneth Ct BH23 47 C7
Kennington Rd BH17 37 E5
Kensington Dr BH2 4 B2
Kensington Pk SO41 51 D3
Kent Rd BH12 38 D6
Kenyon Cl BH15 37 F6
Kenyon Rd BH15 37 G6
Keppel Cl BH24 19 E4
Kerley Rd BH2 4 C5
Kestrel Cl, Ferndown BH22 23 G1
Kestrel Cl, Poole BH16 34 D2
Kestrel Ct BH24 18 C4
Kestrel Dr BH23 60 D1
Keswick Ct BH25 48 C2
Keswick Rd, Bournemouth BH5 58 A3
Keswick Rd, New Milton BH25 48 C2
Keswick Way BH31 7 B3
Keverstone Ct BH1 57 F3
Keyes Cl, Christchurch BH23 60 D2
Keyes Cl, Poole BH12 39 E4
Keyhaven Rd SO41 51 F3
Keysworth Av BH25 49 A7
Keysworth Rd BH16 35 E5
Khyber Rd BH12 54 C2
Kilmarnock Rd BH9 40 C4
Kilmington Way BH23 47 A7
Kiln Cl BH21 27 D6
Kiln Way BH31 7 F4
Kimber Rd BH11 39 E1
Kimberley Cl BH23 43 E5
Kimberley Rd, Bournemouth BH6 58 C2
Kimberley Rd, Poole BH14 54 A4
Kimmeridge Av BH12 38 B5
Kinellar Heights BH4 55 H2
King Cl BH24 15 H3
King Edward Av BH9 40 C2
King Edward Ct BH9 40 C2
King George Av BH9 40 C2
King George Mobile Home Pk BH25 49 A6
King John Av BH11 30 C5
King John Cl BH11 30 C5
King Richard Dr BH11 30 C6
King St BH21 20 D4
Kingcup Cl BH18 36 A2
Kingfisher Cl, Bournemouth BH6 58 D1
Kingfisher Cl, Ferndown BH22 14 C4
Kingfisher Way, Christchurch BH23 60 D2
Kingfisher Way, Ringwood BH24 19 E2
Kingland Cres BH15 6 C3
Kingland Rd BH15 6 D3
Kings Arms La BH24 18 B5
Kings Arms Row BH24 18 B5
Kings Av, Christchurch BH23 59 F1
Kings Av, Poole BH14 54 C4
Kings Cl, Ferndown BH22 14 A5
Kings Cl, Poole BH15 53 F2
Kings Cres BH14 54 D4
Kings Farm La SO41 50 C3
Kings Park Central Dr BH7 57 G1
Kings Park Dr BH7 41 G6
Kings Park Rd BH7 57 G1
Kings Rd, Bournemouth BH3 40 D6
Kings Rd, New Milton BH25 48 D3
Kingsbere Av BH10 39 G3
Kingsbere Gdns BH23 47 B6
Kingsbere Rd BH15 53 F2
Kingsbridge Rd BH14 54 B3
Kingsbury La BH24 18 B5
Kingsfield BH24 18 C5
Kingsland Ct BH13 63 G1
Kingsley Av BH6 59 G4
Kingsley Cl BH6 59 G4
Kingsley Ho BH9 40 C3
Kingsmill Rd BH17 37 G5
Kingston Rd BH15 6 D1
Kingsway BH22 13 G6
Kingsway Cl BH23 43 F5
Kingswell Cl BH10 40 A2
Kingswell Gdns BH10 39 G2
Kingswell Gro BH10 39 G2
Kingswell Rd BH10 39 G2
Kinross Rd BH3 56 B1
Kinsbourne Av BH10 40 A3
Kinson Av BH15 37 H6
Kinson Cl BH10 31 H5
Kinson Gro BH10 31 H5
Kinson Park Rd BH10 31 H4
Kinson Pottery Ind Est BH14 53 H1
Kinson Rd BH10 31 G6
Kipling Rd BH14 54 A1
Kirby Cl BH15 53 G1
Kirby Way BH6 58 D4
Kirkham Av BH23 43 H2
Kirkway BH18 28 C6
Kitchener Cres BH17 36 C2
Kitchers Cl SO41 64 B4
Kitscroft Rd BH10 31 H5
Kittiwake Cl BH6 58 D1
Kitwalls La SO41 51 D2
Kivernell Pl*, Kivernell Rd SO41 51 C3
Kivernell Rd SO41 51 C3
Kiwi Cl BH15 53 G3
Knapp Cl BH23 43 G6
Knapp Mill Av BH23 43 G5
Knightcrest Pk SO41 50 C5
Knighton Heath Cl BH11 30 D6
Knighton Heath Ind Est BH11 38 D2
Knighton Heath Rd BH11 30 D6
Knighton La BH21 30 C3
Knighton Pk BH25 47 F7
Knights Rd BH11 30 C6
Knightsbridge Ct BH2 4 C5
Knightstone Gro BH22 14 A4
Knightwood Cl BH23 45 H6
Knobcrook Rd BH21 20 D3
Knole Ct BH1 57 F3
Knole Gdns BH1 57 F2
Knole Rd BH1 57 F2
Knoll Gdns BH24 15 H2
Knoll La BH21 26 C3
Knoll Manor BH2 4 D1
Knowland Dr SO41 51 E2
Knowles Cl BH23 44 B6
Knowlton Gdns BH9 40 D1
Knowlton Rd BH17 37 G3
Knyveton Ho BH1 5 H2
Knyveton Rd BH1 5 H2
Kyrchil La BH21 21 G2
Kyrchil Way BH21 21 G2

Labrador Dr BH15 6 D5
Laburnum Cl, Ferndown BH22 23 G2
Laburnum Cl, Verwood BH31 7 F3
Laburnum Dr SO41 50 B5
Laburnum Ho BH10 32 B6
Lacey Cres BH15 38 A6
Lacy Cl BH21 21 E2
Lacy Dr BH21 21 E2
Ladysmith Cl BH23 60 B1
Lagado Cl BH14 62 D1
Lagland Ct BH15 6 C4
Lagland St BH15 6 B5
Lagoon Cl BH14 54 A6
Lagoon Rd BH14 54 A6
Laidlaw Cl BH12 39 G5
Lake Av BH15 35 F8
Lake Cres BH15 52 A4
Lake Dr BH15 35 E8
Lake Grove Rd BH25 48 B3
Lake Rd, Bournemouth BH11 31 G5
Lake Rd, Poole BH15 35 F8
Lake Rd, Verwood BH31 7 D4
Lakeside BH24 19 F6
Lakeside Rd BH13 55 F5
Lakeview Dr BH24 19 F5
Lakewood Rd BH23 47 A6
Lambs Cl BH17 36 D3
Lambs Green La BH21 20 A6
Lampton Gdns BH9 40 B3
Lanark Cl BH15 52 A5
Lancaster Cl, Broadstone BH18 28 B5
Lancaster Cl, Christchurch BH23 61 F1
Lancaster Dr, Broadstone BH18 28 A5
Lancaster Dr, Verwood BH31 7 B3
Lancer Cl BH23 43 F6
Lander Cl BH15 6 D5
Landford Gdns BH8 41 G2
Landford Way BH8 41 F2
Landseer Rd BH4 55 G3
Langdon Ct BH14 54 C2
Langdon Rd BH14 54 B2
Langham Ct BH23 43 F4
Langley Chase BH24 16 A2
Langley Rd, Christchurch BH23 45 H4
Langley Rd, Poole BH14 55 E2
Langside Av BH12 39 F5
Langton Cl BH25 49 C6

Langton Rd BH7 57 H2
Lansdell Ct BH15 53 G3
Lansdowne Cres BH1 5 G3
Lansdowne Gdns BH1 5 F1
Lansdowne Ho BH1 5 H3
Lansdowne Rd BH1 5 F1
Lansdowne Rd South
  BH1 56 D3
Lapwing Rd BH21 22 A1
Lara Cl BH8 41 F1
Larch Cl,
  Lymington SO41 50 A1
Larch Cl, Poole BH17 36 A3
Larch Cl,
  Ringwood BH24 16 A3
Larch Way BH22 23 H1
Lark Rd BH23 61 E2
Larks Cl BH22 23 G1
Larks Rise BH22 23 G1
Larksfield Av BH9 41 E1
Larkshill Cl BH25 48 C3
Lascelles Ct BH7 58 B2
Lascelles Rd BH7 58 B2
Latch Farm Av BH23 44 C4
Latimer Rd BH9 40 B5
Latimers Cl BH23 47 A5
Laundry La SO41 51 F3
Laurel Cl,
  Christchurch BH23 45 G5
Laurel Cl,
  Lymington SO41 50 A1
Laurel Cl,
  Ringwood BH24 15 G2
Laurel Cl,
  Wimborne BH21 26 E4
Laurel Dr BH18 28 D6
Laurel Gdns BH18 28 D6
Laurel La BH24 15 G3
Lavender Cl BH31 7 F3
Lavender Rd,
  Bournemouth BH8 33 G6
Lavender Rd,
  Lymington SO41 50 A2
Lavender Walk BH8 33 G6
Lavender Way BH18 27 F7
Lavinia Rd BH12 38 B5
Lawford Rd BH9 40 C1
Lawn Cl SO41 51 F3
Lawn Ct BH2 4 A2
Lawn Rd SO41 51 F3
Lawn Vw BH25 46 F2
Lawns Cl BH21 22 B3
Lawns Rd BH21 22 B2
Lawrence Ct BH8 57 E1
Lawrence Dr BH13 54 D6
Lawrence Rd BH24 19 F2
Lawson Rd BH12 38 B6
Layard Dr BH21 29 F2
Laymoor La BH21 22 C3
Layton Rd BH12 54 C2
Le Patourel Cl BH23 60 B1
Lea Way BH11 30 D4
Leamington Rd BH9 40 C5
Leaphill Rd BH7 58 B2
Learoyd Rd BH17 37 F5
Lechlade Gdns BH7 37 F5
Ledbury Rd BH23 60 C3
Ledgard Ct BH14 54 A3
Leedam Rd BH10 32 A6
Lees Cl BH23 42 D2
Leeson Dr BH22 54 D3
Leeson Rd BH7 41 H6
Legg La BH21 21 E4
Legion Cl BH15 52 A5
Legion Rd BH15 52 A5
Leicester Rd BH13 54 D3
Leiderbach Dr BH31 7 F4
Leigh Cl BH21 21 F4
Leigh Common BH21 21 G4
Leigh Gdns BH21 21 F4
Leigh La BH21 21 G3
Leigh Rd,
  New Milton BH25 48 B3
Leigh Rd,
  Wimborne BH21 21 E4
Leigham Vale Rd BH6 58 D3
Lentham Cl BH17 37 F3
Leslie Cl,
  Bournemouth BH9 40 B5
Leslie Rd, Poole BH14 53 H4
Leven Av BH4 4 A1
Leven Cl BH4 4 A1
Levets La BH15 6 B4
Lewens Cl BH21 21 E4
Lewens La BH21 21 E4
Lewesdon Dr BH18 28 B6
Leybourne Av BH10 31 H5,6
Leybourne Cl BH10 31 H5
Leydene Av BH8 41 H4

Leydene Cl BH8 41 H4
Leyland Rd BH12 38 D3
Leyside BH23 60 C1
Liberty Cl BH21 8 D6
Liberty Ct*,
  Dragoon Way BH23 43 F6
Library Rd,
  Bournemouth BH9 40 B4
Library Rd,
  Ferndown BH22 24 A3
Library Rd,
  Poole BH12 54 D2
Lights Cl BH23 43 G6
Lilac Cl BH24 18 D4
Lilliput Rd BH14 62 C1
Lime Cl BH15 53 G1
Lime Gro SO41 50 B5
Limited Rd BH23 40 C3
Lin Brook Dr BH24 19 E1
Linbrook Almshouses
  BH24 19 E1
Linbrook Ct BH24 18 C3
Linbrook Vw BH24 19 H1
Lincoln Av,
  Bournemouth BH1 57 F1
Lincoln Av,
  Christchurch BH23 43 F4
Lincoln Rd BH12 38 C6
Lindbergh Rd BH21 23 F1
Linden Cl BH24 32 A1
Linden Ct*,
  Linden Gdns BH24 18 C4
Linden Gdns BH24 18 C4
Linden Rd,
  Bournemouth BH9 40 C1
Linden Rd,
  Ferndown BH22 31 H1
Linden Rd, Poole BH12 54 B3
Lindsay Rd BH13 55 F3
Lindsay Manor BH13 55 F3
Lindsay Pk BH13 55 F3
Lindsay Rd BH13 55 E3
Lindum Ct BH13 55 F2
Lineside BH23 44 A5
Linford BH24 19 H1
Linford Cl BH25 48 C3
Linford Ho BH24 19 H1
Linford Rd BH24 19 E3
Ling Rd BH12 38 A4
Lingdale Rd BH6 58 D2
Lingwood Av BH23 60 C2
Linhorns La BH25 48 C1
Link Rd BH24 19 E3
Link Rise BH24 26 F4
Links Dr BH23 42 D5
Links Rd BH14 54 C5
Links View Av BH14 54 D5
Linkside Av BH18 41 H4
Linmead Dr BH11 31 F5
Linnet Cl BH24 19 F6
Linnet Cl BH25 48 A4
Linnet Rd BH17 36 A4
Linthorpe Rd BH15 53 G2
Linwood Rd BH9 40 D6
Lionheart Cl BH11 30 C6
Lions Cl BH5 6 D1
Lions Hill Way BH24 15 E2
Lions La BH24 15 F2
Lions Wood BH24 15 G2
Litchford Rd BH23 48 D3
Little Barrs Dr BH25 48 C3
Little Burn SO41 64 C4
Little Cl, Poole BH14 62 D2
Little Ct, Poole BH14 62 D2
Little Dewlands BH31 7 A2
Little Forest Mansions
  BH1 5 F4
Little Forest Rd BH4 56 A1
Little Lonnen BH21 11 H6
Littlecroft Av BH9 41 E2
Littlecroft Rd BH12 54 A1
Littledown Av BH7 41 G6
Littledown Dr BH7 41 G6
Littlemead Cl BH17 36 B5
Littlemoor Av BH11 38 C1
Livingstone Rd,
  Bournemouth BH5 58 B3
Livingstone Rd,
  Christchurch BH23 60 B1
Livingstone Rd,
  Poole BH12 38 A6
Livingstone Rd,
  Wimborne BH21 21 F4
Llewellin Cl BH16 34 E2
Llewellin Cl BH16 34 E2
Loader Cl BH9 40 D4
Loch Rd BH14 54 D2
Locksley Dr BH22 23 H6
Lockyers Dr BH22 24 C2
Lockyers Rd BH21 28 A2

Loders Cl BH17 37 E1
Lodge Rd BH14 54 D3
Lodge Rd BH14 54 D3
Lodge Rd,
  Christchurch BH23 43 E5
Lodge Rd,
  Wimborne BH21 11 H1
Loewy Cres BH12 38 C2
Lombard Av BH6 58 C5
Lombardy Rd BH31 7 E3
Lone Pine Dr BH22 24 B6
Lone Pine Pk BH22 24 B6
Lone Pine Way BH22 24 B6
Long La BH21 11 F6
Long Rd BH10 31 H6
Longacre Dr BH22 23 H4
Longbarrow Cl BH8 42 A4
Longespee Rd BH21 29 F2
Longfield Dr,
  Bournemouth BH11 31 F4
Longfield Dr,
  Ferndown BH22 32 B2
Longfield Rd SO41 50 C3
Longfleet Dr BH21 29 F6
Longfleet Rd BH15 6 D2
Longfleet Gdns BH25 46 F4
Longmeadow Ind Est
  BH21 8 B5
Longmeadow La BH17 36 A3
Lonnen Rd BH21 11 H6
Lonnen Wood Cl BH21 11 H6
Lonsdale Rd BH3 40 B6
Loraine Av BH23 47 D6
Lord Cl BH17 37 H5
Lorne Park Rd BH1 5 F3
Love La SO41 50 D3
Lower Ashley Rd BH25 48 E4
Lower Blandford Rd
  BH18 36 C1
Lower Common Rd
  BH21 8 C5
Lower Golf Links Rd
  BH18 28 D5
Lower Mead End Rd
  SO41 64 A6
Lowther Gdns BH8 57 E1
Lowther Rd BH8 56 D1
Lucas Rd,
  Lower Hamworthy
  BH15 6 A6
Lucas Rd, Poole BH12 54 B1
Lucerne Av BH6 58 D3
Lucerne Rd SO41 51 E3
Luckham Cl BH9 41 E3
Luckham Gdns BH9 41 E2
Luckham Pl BH9 41 E3
Luckham Rd BH9 41 E3
Luckham Rd East BH9 41 E2
Lulworth Av BH15 52 A5
Lulworth Cl BH15 52 A5
Lulworth Cres BH15 35 F8
Lumby Dr BH24 19 E3
Lumby Dr Caravan Pk
  BH24 19 E3
Luscombe Rd BH14 50 B4
Luther Rd BH9 40 C4
Lych Gate Ct BH24 19 E6
Lydford Gdns BH11 38 D3
Lydford Rd BH11 39 F2
Lydlinch Cl BH22 32 A1
Lydwell Cl BH11 31 E5
Lyell Rd BH12 54 B1
Lyme Cres BH23 47 A7
Lymefields SO41 51 E2
Lymington Rd,
  Christchurch BH23 45 G6
Lymington Rd,
  Everton SO41 50 B5
Lymington Rd,
  New Milton BH25 50 B6
Lymore La SO41 51 F1
Lymore Valley SO41 51 F1
Lyndale Cl SO41 51 E3
Lyndhurst Rd,
  Brockenhampton BH23 44 C1
Lyndhurst Rd,
  Christchurch BH23 45 E5
Lyndon Ct BH23 43 F4
Lynes La BH24 18 B5
Lynn Rd BH17 37 H4
Lynric Cl BH25 49 B8
Lynton Cres BH23 42 D2
Lynwood Cl BH22 24 A2
Lynwood Dr BH21 29 G2
Lyon Av BH25 48 C4
Lyon Rd BH12 38 D3
Lysander Cl BH23 45 F6
Lystra Rd BH9 40 C2
Lytchett Dr BH18 36 B2

Lytchett Minster By-Pass
  BH16 34 A4
Lytchett Way BH16 34 D4
Lytham Rd BH18 36 C2
Lytton Rd BH1 57 H5

Mabey Av BH10 39 H2
MacAndrew Rd BH13 63 F1
Macaulay Rd BH18 28 C6
Maclaren Rd BH9 40 C2
Maclean Rd BH11 39 E2
Madeira Rd,
  Bournemouth BH1 5 E3
Madeira Rd,
  Poole BH14 54 C2
Madeline Cl BH12 38 A6
Madeline Cres BH12 38 A6
Madison Av BH1 57 G1
Magdalen La BH23 59 G1
Magna Cl BH11 31 E4
Magna Gdns BH11 31 E4
Magna Rd BH11,21 30 A2
Magnolia Cl,
  Bournemouth BH6 59 G3
Magnolia Cl,
  Verwood BH31 7 F4
Magnolia Ho BH10 32 C6
Magpie Cl BH8 41 F2
Magpie Gro BH25 49 A5
Mags Barrow BH22 24 B6
Maidment Cl BH11 38 D1
Majorca Mansions BH2 4 B3
Malan Cl BH17 37 F5
Malcomb Cl BH6 59 F5
Mallard Cl,
  Bournemouth BH8 41 F3
Mallard Cl,
  Christchurch BH23 60 D1
Mallard Cl,
  Lymington SO41 50 C2
Mallard Rd,
  Bournemouth BH8 41 F4
Mallard Rd,
  Wimborne BH21 21 H1
Mallory Cl BH23 44 D5
Mallow Cl,
  Broadstone BH18 36 A2
Mallow Cl,
  Christchurch BH23 45 F5
Malmesbury Cl BH23 59 G2
Malmesbury Ct BH8 57 E1
Malmesbury Park Pl
  BH8 57 F1
Malmesbury Park Rd
  BH8 57 E1
Malmesbury Rd BH24 15 G3
Maloren Way BH22 14 C5
Malthouse BH15 6 B4
Malvern Cl BH9 40 C2
Malvern Ct BH9 40 D3
Malvern Ct*,
  Dorset BH23 44 C5
Malvern Rd BH9 40 C2
Manchester Rd SO41 64 B4
Mandalay Cl BH31 7 B4
Mandale Cl BH11 39 F1
Mandale Rd BH11 39 E1
Manderley SO41 51 E4
Manning Av BH23 45 F5
Mannings Heath Rd
  BH12 38 A3
Mannington Pl BH2 4 B4
Mannington Way BH22 13 H4
Manor Av BH12 38 B4
Manor Cl,
  Ferndown BH22 24 A3
Manor Cl,
  Lymington SO41 51 D2
Manor Ct BH24 18 C4
Manor Farm Cl BH25 49 A5
Manor Farm Rd BH10 31 G4
Manor Gdns,
  Ringwood BH24 18 C4
Manor Gdns,
  Verwood BH31 7 B2
Manor Pk BH15 52 D2
Manor Rd,
  Bournemouth BH1 5 H3
Manor Rd,
  Christchurch BH23 59 F1
Manor Rd,
  Lymington SO41 51 D2
Manor Rd,
  New Milton BH25 48 C4
Manor Rd,
  Ringwood BH24 18 D4
Manor Rd,
  Verwood BH31 7 B2
Manor Way BH31 7 C2

Mansel Cl BH12 39 H5
Mansfield Av BH14 54 B2
Mansfield Cl,
  Ferndown BH22 24 A6
Mansfield Cl,
  Poole BH14 54 B2
Mansfield Rd,
  Bournemouth BH9 40 B4
Mansfield Rd,
  Poole BH14 54 B3
Mansfield Rd,
  Ringwood BH24 18 C4
Manton Cl BH15 52 A3
Manton Rd BH15 52 A3
Maple Cl,
  Christchurch BH23 47 A7
Maple Cl,
  New Milton BH25 49 C8
Maple Dr BH22 23 H1
Maple Rd,
  Bournemouth BH9 40 B4
Maple Rd, Poole BH15 6 D2
Mapperton Cl BH17 37 H3
Marabout Cl BH23 44 B6
Marchwood Rd BH10 39 H1
Margards La BH31 7 A3
Marian Rd BH21 27 E6
Marian Rd BH21 27 E6
Marianne Rd,
  Poole BH12 39 H5
Marianne Rd,
  Wimborne BH21 21 H1
Marie Cl BH12 38 C6
Marina Cl BH5 57 G3
Marina Ct BH5 57 G3
Marina Dr BH14 54 A5
Marina Towers BH5 57 G3
Marina Vw BH23 59 F2
Marine Cl BH25 47 E8
Marine Dr BH25 49 A8
Marine Dr East BH25 49 B8
Marine Dr West BH25 47 E8
Marine Rd BH6 58 D4
Mariners Ct BH23 60 D2
Market Cl BH15 6 B4
Market Pl BH24 18 B4
Market St BH15 6 B4
Market Way BH21 21 E5
Markham Av BH10 32 A4
Markham Cl BH10 32 A4
Markham Rd BH9 40 C5
Marks La BH25 48 B1
Marks Rd BH9 40 C1
Marlborough Ct,
  Poole BH12 55 F3
Marlborough Ct,
  Wimborne BH21 20 D3
Marlborough Pl BH21 21 E3
Marlborough Rd,
  Bournemouth BH4 4 A4
Marlborough Rd,
  Poole BH14 54 B3
Marley Av BH25 48 A3
Marley Cl BH25 48 A4
Marline Rd BH12 54 C1
Marlott Rd BH15 53 E2
Marlow Dr BH23 42 D2
Marlpit Dr BH23 47 B5
Marmion Grn BH23 60 C1
Marnhull Rd BH15 53 F2
Marpet Cl BH11 31 E5
Marquis Way BH11 30 C5
Marryat Ct,
  Christchurch BH23 47 C7
Marryat Ct,
  New Milton BH25 48 A3
Marryat Rd BH25 48 A4
Marsh Cl BH6 58 D4
Marsh Ditch BH23 59 G2
Marsh La,
  Christchurch BH23 60 A1
Marsh La,
  Fairmile BH23 43 F3
Marsh La, Poole BH16 34 B2
Marshal Rd BH17 36 D3
Marshall Rd BH21 21 G1
Marshlands Cl BH23 60 A2
Marshwood Av BH17 37 G2
Marston Cl BH25 48 C2
Marston Gro BH23 45 H4
Marston Rd,
  New Milton BH25 48 C2
Marston Rd,
  Poole BH15 6 B4
Martello Rd BH13 63 G1
Martello Rd BH13 63 G1
Martello Pk BH13 63 G1
Martello Rd South
  BH13 55 E6
Martello Towers BH13 63 G1

73

Martin Cl BH17 36 A5
Martin Rd BH12 54 D1
Martindale Av BH21 22 A4
Martingale Cl BH16 34 F3
Martins Cl BH22 24 A1
Martins Dr BH22 24 B1
Martins Hill Cl BH23 44 A4
Martins Hill La BH23 44 A5
Martins Way BH22 24 A1
Marwell Cl BH7 42 A6
Mary La BH22 14 A4
Mary Mitchell Cl*, Kings Arms La BH24 18 B5
Maryland Ct SO41 51 B3
Maryland Gdns SO41 51 C3
Maryland Rd BH16 35 E5
Masterson Cl BH23 44 B6
Matchams La BH23 17 B1
Matlock Rd BH22 23 H5
Maundeville Cres BH23 42 D6
Maundeville Rd BH23 43 E6
Maureen Cl BH12 38 A5
Maurice Rd BH8 41 F5
Mavis Rd BH9 40 D3
Maxwell Rd, Bournemouth BH9 40 C5
Maxwell Rd, Broadstone BH18 27 F7
Maxwell Rd, Poole BH13 63 F1
May Gdns, Bournemouth BH11 38 D1
May Gdns, Christchurch BH23 47 C5
Mayfair BH4 55 G4
Mayfair Gdns BH11 31 F6
Mayfield Av BH14 54 D4
Mayfield Cl BH22 23 H2
Mayfield Dr BH22 23 H2
Mayfield Rd BH9 40 C3
Mayfield Way BH22 23 H2
Mayford Rd BH12 39 G6
McIntyre Rd BH23 17 A4
Mckinley Rd BH4 55 H5
McWilliam Cl BH12 39 G5
McWilliam Rd BH9 40 C2
Mead Cl BH18 36 C3
Mead End Rd SO41 64 A5
Meadow Bank BH16 34 E2
Meadow Cl, Christchurch BH23 64 B3
Meadow Cl, Ferndown BH22 32 A1
Meadow Cl, Ringwood BH24 18 D3
Meadow Court Cl BH9 40 C2
Meadow Ct, Verwood BH31 7 D4
Meadow Ct, Wimborne BH21 21 E4
Meadow Farm La BH21 26 F2
Meadow Gro BH31 7 D3
Meadow La BH23 44 A3
Meadow Rd, New Milton BH25 48 C3
Meadow Rd, Ringwood BH24 18 D3
Meadow Rise BH18 28 A5
Meadow View Rd BH11 30 D6
Meadow Way, New Milton BH25 49 C8
Meadow Way, Ringwood BH24 18 D3
Meadow Way, Verwood BH31 7 D4
Meadowland BH23 60 C2
Meadows Cl BH16 34 E2
Meadows Dr BH16 34 E2
Meadowsweet Rd BH17 36 A4
Medina Way BH23 61 F1
Medlar Cl BH23 44 A4
Medway Rd BH22 24 D2
Meeting House La BH24 18 B4
Melbourne Rd, Bournemouth BH8 57 F1
Melbourne Rd, Christchurch BH23 43 E4
Melbury Av BH12 38 C5
Melbury Cl BH22 23 H4
Mellstock Rd BH15 53 E2
Melrose Ct BH25 48 E4
Melton Ct BH13 55 E3
Melverley Gdns BH21 21 E3
Melville Gdns BH9 40 B4
Melville Rd BH9 40 B4
Mendip Cl, New Milton BH25 49 D5
Mendip Cl, Verwood BH31 7 C3
Mendip Ct*, Dorset Rd BH23 44 C5
Mendip Rd BH31 7 C2
Mentone Rd BH14 53 H3
Meon Rd BH7 58 B1
Meredith Cl BH23 44 B6
Meriden Cl BH13 63 G2
Merino Way BH22 14 B5
Merlewood Cl BH2 4 D1
Merley Dr BH23 47 B7
Merley Gdns BH21 29 F2
Merley La BH21 29 E1
Merley Park Rd BH21 28 A2
Merley Ways BH21 21 E6
Merlin Cl BH24 19 F6
Merlin Way BH23 61 E2
Mermaid Ct BH5 57 G3
Merriefield Av BH18 28 D5
Merriefield Cl BH18 28 D4
Merriefield Dr BH18 28 D5
Merrifield BH21 21 G1
Merritown La BH23 33 G3
Merrivale Av BH6 59 E3
Merrow Av BH12 39 G6
Merryfield Cl, Christchurch BH23 64 B2
Merryfield Cl, Verwood BH31 7 C2
Merryfield La BH10 39 H1
Merryweather Est BH24 19 E4
Merton Ct BH23 47 C7
Merton Gro BH24 18 C4
Methuen Cl BH8 57 E2
Methuen Rd, Bournemouth BH8 56 D1
Methuen Rd, Poole BH17 36 D3
Meyrick Cl BH23 64 B3
Meyrick Park Cres BH3 56 B1
Meyrick Park Mansions BH2 4 D2
Meyrick Rd BH1 5 G3
Michelgrove Rd BH5 57 G3
Michelmersh Grn BH8 41 F2
Mickleham Cl BH12 39 G5
Middle La BH24 18 C5
Middle Rd, Bournemouth BH10 31 G6
Middle Rd, Poole BH15 53 F1
Middle Rd, Sway SO41 64 B5
Middle Rd, Tiptoe SO41 64 A6
Middlebere Cres BH16 35 E6
Middlehill Dr BH21 22 A2
Middlehill Rd BH21 21 G1
Middleton Mews BH25 49 B6
Middleton Rd, Bournemouth BH9 40 B2
Middleton Rd, Ringwood BH24 18 D3
Midland Rd BH9 40 C4
Midway Path BH13 62 C6
Midwood Av BH8 41 H3
Milborne Cres BH12 38 D5
Milbourne Rd BH22 23 H2
Milburn Cl BH4 55 H3
Milburn Rd BH4 55 G3
Milestone Rd BH15 53 E1
Milford Cl BH22 14 C4
Milford Cres SO41 51 E3
Milford Ct SO41 51 E3
Milford Dr BH11 31 E5
Milford Rd, Lymington SO41 50 B5
Milford Rd, New Milton BH25 49 C6
Milford Trading Est SO41 51 E3
Mill Cotts BH21 26 C1
Mill Hill Cl BH14 54 A4
Mill La, Christchurch BH23 47 D6
Mill La, Hurn BH23 17 B5
Mill La, Poole BH14 54 A4
Mill La, Wimborne BH21 20 D4
Mill Mdw SO41 51 D3
Mill Rd BH23 43 G6
Mill Rd North BH8 41 G1
Mill Rd South BH8 41 F2
Mill St BH21 26 C1
Miller Cl BH25 48 D3
Miller Rd BH23 44 B6
Millfield, New Milton BH25 46 F4
Millfield, Poole BH17 36 C6
Millhams Cl BH10 31 G4
Millhams Dr BH10 31 G4
Millhams Rd BH10 31 F4
Millhams St BH23 59 H1
Millhams St North BH23 59 H1
Millstream Cl, Poole BH17 36 B5
Millstream Cl, Wimborne BH21 20 D4
Millstream Trading Est BH24 18 C6
Millyford Cl BH25 47 E7
Milne Rd BH17 36 C3
Milner Rd BH4 55 H5
Milton Cl BH14 54 C4
Milton Ct BH22 23 H3
Milton Gro BH25 49 C5
Milton Mead BH25 49 A5
Milton Rd, Bournemouth BH8 56 C1
Milton Rd, Poole BH14 54 C4
Milton Rd, Wimborne BH21 20 D2
Milverton Cl BH23 47 A5
Mimosa Av BH21 29 F2
Minstead Rd BH10 39 H1
Minster Vw BH21 21 E3
Minster Way BH16 34 D2
Minterne Grange BH14 62 D1
Minterne Rd, Bournemouth BH9 40 D2
Minterne Rd, Christchurch BH23 60 C2
Minterne Rd, Poole BH14 62 D1
Mission Rd BH18 36 C2
Mitchell Cl BH25 49 B7
Mitchell Rd, Poole BH17 37 G5
Mitchell Rd, Wimborne BH21 23 F1
Moat Ct BH4 55 G2
Moat La BH25 49 B6
Moffat Rd BH23 60 B1
Molefields SO41 51 E3
Molyneaux Rd BH25 48 E4
Monaco Ct BH9 41 E4
Moneyfly Rd BH31 7 E3
Monks Cl BH22 14 D6
Monks Way BH11 30 C5
Monkshood Cl BH23 45 F5
Monkswell Grn BH23 60 A2
Monkton Cl BH22 24 A2
Monkton Cres BH12 38 D5
Monkworthy Dr BH24 15 H1
Monmouth Cl BH31 7 E4
Monmouth Dr BH31 7 D4
Monsal Av BH22 23 H5
Montacute Way BH21 29 F3
Montagu Pk BH23 47 B7
Montagu Rd BH23 47 C7
Montague Rd BH5 58 B4
Monteray Dr SO41 50 B1
Montgomery Av BH11 39 G1
Montrose Cl BH31 7 C2
Montrose Dr BH10 39 G3
Moonrakers Way BH23 45 H5
Moor Rd BH18 28 C6
Moor View Rd BH15 37 G6
Moorcroft Av BH23 44 A3
Moordown Cl BH9 40 C1
Moore Av BH11 39 F1
Moore Cl BH25 49 A6
Moorfield Gro BH9 40 C3
Moorfields Rd BH13 63 F1
Moorings Cl BH15 52 B5
Moorland Av BH25 49 A6
Moorland Cres BH16 34 D3
Moorland Par BH16 34 D3
Moorland Rd BH1 57 F2
Moorland Way BH16 34 D3
Moorlands Rd, Ferndown BH22 14 A4
Moorlands Rd, Verwood BH31 7 C1
Moorlands Rise BH22 14 B3
Moorlea BH8 5 H1
Moors Cl BH23 17 B4
Moorside Cl BH11 39 G1
Moorside Gdns BH11 39 F2
Moorside Rd, Bournemouth BH11 39 F2
Moorside Rd, Ferndown BH22 14 A5
Moorside Rd, Wimborne BH21 27 F5
Moorvale Rd BH9 40 D2
Morant Rd BH24 18 D2
Moray Ct BH21 20 D3
Morden Av BH22 23 H5
Morden Rd BH9 40 B3
Moreton Rd BH9 32 D6
Morley Cl, Bournemouth BH5 58 B3
Morley Cl, Christchurch BH23 43 H2
Morley Rd BH7 58 A2
Mornish Rd BH13 55 E4
Morris Rd BH17 37 F5
Morrison Av BH12 39 E6
Mortimer Cl BH23 61 E2
Mortimer Rd BH8 41 E4
Mossley Av BH12 39 E4
Motcombe Rd BH13 55 F5
Mount Av BH25 49 C5
Mount Cl BH25 49 C6
Mount Grace Dr BH14 62 D2
Mount Heatherbank BH1 4 D3
Mount Pleasant Dr, Bournemouth BH8 41 H3
Mount Pleasant Dr, Christchurch BH23 64 D1
Mount Pleasant La BH24 18 C4
Mount Pleasant Rd BH15 6 D3
Mount Rd, Bournemouth BH11 39 F1
Mount Rd, Poole BH14 54 A2
Mount Stuart Rd BH5 57 G4
Mountbatten Cl BH23 60 D2
Mountbatten Ct*, Raleigh Cl BH25 48 A4
Mountbatten Dr BH22 23 H3
Mountbatten Gdns BH8 42 A3
Mountbatten Rd BH13 55 G5
Mountjoy Cl BH21 29 H1
Mude Gdns BH23 60 D3
Mudeford BH23 60 C3
Mudeford Green Cl BH23 60 D3
Mudeford La BH23 60 B1
Mulberry Gro SO41 50 B5
Mullins Cl BH12 39 H4
Munster Rd BH14 54 C4
Murley Rd BH9 40 D4
Muscliffe La BH9 32 D6
Muscliffe Rd BH9 40 C4
Myrtle Cl SO41 50 A1
Myrtle Rd BH8 41 F6

Nada Rd BH23 45 G4
Nairn Rd, Bournemouth BH3 40 B6
Nairn Rd, Poole BH13 63 E2
Naish Est BH25 47 D7
Naish Rd BH25 47 F7
Namu Rd BH9 40 A4
Nansen Av BH15 53 F1
Napier Rd BH15 35 C7
Narrow La BH24 19 F3
Naseby Rd BH9 40 D3
Nathan Gdns BH15 35 F7
Nea Cl BH23 45 G5
Nea Rd BH23 45 H6
Neacroft Cl BH25 47 E7
Needles Ct SO41 51 C3
Needles Point SO41 51 D4
Nelson Cl BH25 48 A4
Nelson Ct BH15 6 C4
Nelson Dr BH23 60 D2
Nelson Rd BH12 55 F2
Netherhall Gdns BH4 55 H3
Netherwood Pl BH21 20 C3
Netley Cl BH15 37 H6
Nettleton Cl BH17 37 F5
New Borough Rd BH21 21 E5
New Cotts BH23 33 F3
New Ct BH24 18 B5
New Harbour Rd BH15 6 A6
New Harbour Rd South BH15 6 A6
New Harbour Rd West BH15 52 C6
New La, Lymington SO41 51 F4
New La, New Milton BH25 48 A1
New Merrifield BH21 21 G1
New Orch BH15 6 B4
New Park Rd BH6 58 C3
New Quay Rd BH15 6 A5
New Rd, Ferndown BH10,22 24 A4
New Rd, Poole BH12 54 C1
New St, Poole BH15 6 B4
New St, Ringwood BH24 18 C6
New Valley Rd SO41 51 D3
Newbury Dr BH10 40 A3
Newcombe Rd, Bournemouth BH6 59 E2
Newcombe Rd, Ferndown BH22 14 A4
Newcroft Gdns BH23 43 G6
Newfields Bsns Pk BH17 37 E4
Newfoundland Dr BH15 6 C4
Newlands Rd, Bournemouth BH7 58 A1
Newlands Rd, Christchurch BH23 44 D6
Newlands Rd, New Milton BH25 49 C5
Newlands Way BH18 27 F7
Newlyn Way BH12 38 D6
Newmans Cl BH22 14 A1
Newmans La BH22 13 H1
Newmorton Rd BH9 32 C6
Newstead Rd BH6 58 D4
Newton Morrell BH14 54 C4
Newton Rd, New Milton BH25 49 C6
Newton Rd, Poole BH13 63 F1
Newtown Bsns Centre BH12 38 A5
Newtown La, Verwood BH31 7 C3
Newtown La, Wimborne BH21 26 F2
Newtown Rd BH31 7 D2,3
Nicholas Cl BH23 47 C5
Nicholas Gdns BH10 39 H3
Nicholson Cl BH17 37 G5
Nightingale Cl BH31 7 D3
Nightingale La BH15 6 B3
Nightjar Cl BH17 36 A5
Nimrod Way BH21 23 E2
Noble Cl BH11 39 E3
Noel Rd BH10 39 G3
Noon Gdns BH31 7 E2
Noon Hill Dr BH31 7 E2
Noon Hill Rd BH31 7 E2
Norcliffe Cl BH11 39 G2
Norfolk Av BH23 43 F4
Norleywood BH23 47 A7
Norman Av BH12 39 E6
Norman Gdns BH12 39 E6
Normandy Cl SO41 64 B5
Normandy Dr BH23 44 B6
Normandy Way BH15 35 F7
Normanhurst Av BH8 41 G4
Normanton Cl BH23 43 E4
Norris Cl BH24 15 G2
Norris Gdns BH25 49 C5
Norrish Rd BH12 54 C2
North Av BH10 31 H4
North East Ind Est BH23 33 H1
North Head SO41 51 B3
North Lodge Rd BH14 54 D3
North Poulner Rd BH24 18 D2
North Rd, Bournemouth BH7 57 H1
North Rd, Poole BH14 53 G3
North St BH15 6 C3
North West Ind Area BH23 33 F2
Northbourne Av BH10 32 A6
Northbourne Gdns BH10 32 A5
Northbourne Pl BH10 32 A5
Northbrook Rd BH18 36 B2
Northcote Rd BH1 5 H1
Northey Rd BH6 59 E2
Northfield Rd, Lymington SO41 51 F3
Northfield Rd, Ringwood BH24 18 C3
Northleigh La BH21 21 G3
Northmead Dr BH17 36 A5
Northmere Dr BH12 39 E6
Northmere Rd BH12 39 E6
Nortoft Rd BH8 40 D6
Norton Cl BH23 60 B1
Norton Rd BH9 40 A4
Norton Way BH15 52 C6
Norway Cl BH9 40 C4
Norwich Av BH2 4 B3
Norwich Av West BH2 4 A3
Norwich Ct BH2 4 B4
Norwich Mansions BH2 4 A3
Norwich Rd BH2 4 B4
Norwood Pl BH5 58 B3
Nouale La BH24 19 F4
Noyce Gdns BH8 42 B4

Nuffield Ind Est BH17 37 E5
Nuffield Rd BH17 36 D5
Nugent Rd BH6 59 F4
Nursery Rd, Bournemouth BH9 40 C2
Nursery Rd, Ringwood BH24 18 C5
Nursling Grn BH8 41 F2
Nuthatch Cl, Ferndown BH22 23 G1
Nuthatch Cl, Poole BH17 36 B5
Nutley Cl BH11 39 E1
Nutley Way BH11 39 E1

Oak Av BH23 42 D6
Oak Cl, Ferndown BH22 32 A2
Oak Cl, Wimborne BH21 27 E5
Oak Gdns SO41 50 B5
Oak La BH24 18 D3
Oak Rd, Bournemouth BH8 41 F6
Oak Rd, New Milton BH25 48 D4
Oak Rd, Poole BH16 34 E4
Oak Tree Par BH23 64 C2
Oakdale Rd BH15 37 F6
Oakdene Cl BH21 21 F4
Oakenbrow SO41 64 A4
Oakfield Rd BH15 53 E1
Oakford Ct BH8 41 F2
Oakhurst Cl BH22 14 B4
Oakhurst La BH22 14 B4
Oakhurst Rd BH22 14 B5
Oakland Walk BH22 32 B1
Oaklands Cl BH31 7 B2
Oakleigh Way BH23 47 A7
Oakley Gdns BH16 34 C2
Oakley Hill BH21 21 E5
Oakley La BH21 21 F6
Oakley Rd BH21 21 F6
Oakley Straight BH21 29 F1
Oakmead Rd BH17 36 B5
Oaks Dr BH24 15 F3
Oaks Mead BH31 7 C2
Oaktree Cl SO41 51 C3
Oakwood Av BH25 48 D3
Oakwood Cl, Bournemouth BH9 40 D3
Oakwood Cl, Ringwood BH24 15 H1
Oakwood Ct BH25 48 C4
Oakwood Rd, Bournemouth BH9 40 D3
Oakwood Rd, Christchurch BH23 47 A5
Oasis Mews BH16 34 C2
Oates Rd BH9 40 B3
Oban Rd BH3 40 B6
Ocean Heights BH5 57 H3
Okeford Rd BH18 36 D2
Old Barn Cl, Christchurch BH23 42 D3
Old Barn Cl, Ringwood BH24 19 E5
Old Barn Farm Rd BH21 8 D6
Old Barn Rd BH23 34 E4
Old Bound Rd BH16 34 E4
Old Bridge Rd BH6 42 D6
Old Christchurch La BH1 5 E3
Old Christchurch Rd, Bournemouth BH1 4 D4
Old Christchurch Rd, Lymington SO41 50 A5
Old Coach Mews BH14 54 A3
Old Coastguard Rd BH13 62 C5
Old Farm Cl BH24 19 F2
Old Farm Rd BH15 37 F6
Old Forge Rd BH21 23 E2
Old Ham La BH21 22 C4
Old Highway Mews BH21 21 F4
Old Kiln Rd BH16 34 E3
Old Manor Cl BH21 21 F4
Old Market Rd BH21 26 A3
Old Mill Ho BH24 18 B5
Old Milton Grn BH25 49 A6
Old Milton Rd BH25 49 B6
Old Mulberry Cl BH10 39 F4
Old Orch BH15 6 B4
Old Pines Cl BH22 24 B4
Old Priory Rd BH6 59 F3
Old Rectory Cl BH21 26 F2
Old Sandpit La BH16 27 B8

Old Sawmill Cl BH31 7 A2
Old School Cl, Ferndown BH22 23 H3
Old School Cl, Poole BH14 53 H3
Old Stacks Gdns BH24 19 E5
Old Town Mews BH15 6 B4
Old Town Mews*, Market Cl BH15 52 D5
Old Vicarage Cl BH10 32 B5
Old Vicarage La SO41 64 C6
Old Wareham Rd, Beacon Hill BH16 27 B8
Old Wareham Rd, Poole BH12 37 H5
Olivers Rd BH21 21 H2
Olivers Way BH21 21 H2
Onslow Gdns BH21 21 E3
Onslow Ho BH21 21 E2
Ophir Gdns BH8 57 E2
Ophir Rd BH8 56 D1
Oratory Gdns BH13 63 G1
Orchard Av BH14 53 G4
Orchard Cl, Christchurch BH23 59 G1
Orchard Cl, Ferndown BH22 24 A3
Orchard Cl, Lymington SO41 51 D2
Orchard Cl, Ringwood BH24 18 C3
Orchard Cl, Wimborne BH21 26 F3
Orchard Ct BH31 7 D3
Orchard Gro BH25 49 B6
Orchard La BH21 26 F3
Orchard Mead BH24 18 C4
Orchard Mews BH23 59 G1
Orchard Mount BH24 18 C4
Orchard St BH2 4 C4
Orchard Walk BH2 4 C4
Orchid Way BH23 60 A1
Orford Cl BH23 42 D1
Ormonde Rd BH13 55 F5
Osborne Ct SO41 51 C3
Osborne Rd, Bournemouth BH9 40 B5
Osborne Rd, New Milton BH25 48 C4
Osborne Rd, Poole BH14 54 A3
Osborne Rd, Wimborne BH21 21 E5
Osprey Cl BH23 60 D3
Oswald Cl BH9 40 B3
Oswald Rd BH9 40 B3
Otter Cl, Poole BH16 34 C4
Otter Cl, Verwood BH31 7 D3
Otter Rd BH15 37 H6
Otterbourne BH2 4 A2
Otters Walk BH25 48 D1
Over Links Dr BH14 54 C5
Overbury Rd BH14 54 B4
Overcliff Dr BH6 59 E5
Overcliff Mansions BH1 5 H4
Overcombe Cl BH17 37 F2
Overstrand Cres SO41 51 E4
Ovington Av BH7 42 C6
Ovington Gdns BH7 42 C6
Owls Rd, Bournemouth BH5 57 G3
Owls Rd, Verwood BH31 7 D3
Oxey Cl BH25 49 B6
Oxford Av BH6 58 B3
Oxford La BH11 31 G5
Oxford Ter BH8 5 G2
Oxford Ter SO41 54 A3

Paddington Cl BH11 38 C1
Paddington Gro BH11 38 C1
Paddock Cl, Poole BH12 38 A6
Paddock Cl, Ringwood BH24 15 H2
Paddock Cl, Wimborne BH21 23 F3
Paddock Gro BH31 7 D3
Padfield Cl BH6 59 E2
Padget Rd BH24 19 F2
Paget Cl BH21 21 H2
Paget Rd BH11 31 F6
Paisley Rd BH6 58 C2
Palfrey Rd BH10 32 A6
Palmer Pl BH25 48 C3
Palmer Rd BH15 52 D2
Palmerston Av BH23 60 B1
Palmerston Cl BH16 34 E3
Palmerston Mews BH1 57 G2

Palmerston Rd, Bournemouth BH1 57 G1
Palmerston Rd, Poole BH14 54 C2
Palmerston Rd, Upton BH16 34 E2
Panorama Rd BH13 62 C6
Pans Corner BH22 24 B5
Paradise St BH15 6 B5
Pardys Hill BH21 26 E2
Parham Cl BH25 48 A4
Parham Rd BH10 39 G3
Parish Rd BH15 53 F3
Park Av BH10 31 H4
Park Cl, Christchurch BH23 44 A2
Park Cl, Lymington SO41 51 E3
Park Cl, New Milton BH25 48 D2
Park Ct, Lymington SO41 51 D3
Park Ct, Poole BH13 55 G4
Park Dr BH31 7 B1
Park Gate Mews BH2 4 B4
Park Gdns BH23 44 E5
Park Homer Dr BH21 21 H2
Park Homer Rd BH21 21 H2
Park La, Bournemouth BH10 32 C6
Park La, Lymington SO41 51 D4
Park La, Wimborne BH21 20 D4
Park Lake Rd BH15 53 F5
Park Pl BH14 53 H3
Park Rd, Ashley BH25 48 D2
Park Rd, Bournemouth BH8 5 F1
Park Rd, Lymington SO41 51 E3
Park Rd, New Milton BH25 49 A6
Park Rd, Poole BH14 53 H3
Park Way BH22 14 A4
Parker Rd BH9 40 C5
Parkers Cl BH24 19 E3
Parkland Dr BH25 49 A6
Parkside, Christchurch BH23 45 G5
Parkside, Ringwood BH24 18 C6
Parkside Gdns BH10 40 A2
Parkside Rd BH14 54 C3
Parkstone Av BH14 54 C3
Parkstone Heights BH14 53 H1
Parkstone Rd BH15 6 D3
Parkview BH2 4 C2
Parkview Mews BH25 48 B4
Parkway Dr BH8 41 G4
Parkwood Rd, Bournemouth BH5 58 A3
Parkwood Rd, Wimborne BH21 21 E4
Parley Cl BH22 32 B2
Parley Green La BH23 33 E3
Parley La BH23 32 D2
Parley Rd BH9 40 C2
Parmiter Dr BH21 21 G4
Parmiter Rd BH21 21 G4
Parmiter Way BH21 21 G4
Parr St BH14 54 A3
Parsonage Barn La BH24 18 C4
Parsonage Rd BH1 5 F4
Partridge Cl BH23 60 D2
Partridge Dr BH14 54 B6
Partridge Grn BH25 48 D1
Partridge Walk BH14 54 B5
Pascoe Cl BH14 54 A2
Patchins Rd BH16 35 D6
Pauncefote Rd BH5 58 A3
Pauntley Rd BH23 60 B2
Pavan Gdns BH10 39 H2
Payne Rd BH22 14 B1
Peace Cl BH23 64 B2
Pear Cl BH12 55 G3
Pear Tree Cl BH23 64 C2
Pearce Av BH14 53 H6
Pearce Gdns BH14 53 H5
Pearce Rd BH16 34 C3
Pearce Smith Ct BH25 49 A8
Pearl Gdns BH10 31 H6
Pearl Rd BH10 31 H6
Pearson Av BH14 54 B2
Pearson Gdns BH10 31 H5
Peckham Av BH25 48 B4
Pedlars Walk BH24 18 B5
Peeks Mews BH6 59 F3

Peel Cl BH12 54 B1
Pegasus Av SO41 50 C3
Pegasus Ct BH1 56 C2
Pelham Cl BH23 60 B1
Pelican Mead BH24 19 E6
Pembroke Ct BH23 47 C7
Pembroke Rd, Bournemouth BH4 55 G4
Pembroke Rd, Poole BH12 38 C6
Penelope Ct BH23 47 C7
Pengelly Av BH10 32 A5
Penn Cl BH25 49 A6
Penn Ct BH22 14 A4
Penn Hill Av BH14 54 C3
Pennant Way BH23 44 D6
Pennine Cl BH22 14 A5
Pennine Way BH31 7 C3
Pennington Cl BH22 14 A5
Pennington Cres BH22 14 A5
Pennington Rd BH22 14 A5
Penny Hedge BH25 49 C7
Penny Way BH23 61 G1
Pennys Walk BH22 24 A3
Pennywell Gdns BH25 48 E3
Penrith Cl BH31 7 B3
Penrith Rd BH5 58 A4
Penrose Rd BH22 24 A3
Percy Rd BH5 57 H3
Peregrine Rd BH23 60 D2
Pergin Cres BH17 36 C5
Pergin Way BH17 36 C5
Perry Gdns BH15 6 C4
Perryfield Gdns BH7 42 B5
Persley Rd BH10 32 A6
Perth Cl BH23 43 E5
Peter Grant Way BH22 23 H3
Peters Cl BH16 34 E4
Peters Rd BH22 24 B5
Petersfield Pl BH7 58 B1
Petersfield Rd BH7 42 B6
Petersham La BH21 11 F1
Petersham Rd BH17 36 B5
Petit Rd BH9 40 D1
Petwyn Cl BH22 24 C2
Peverell Rd BH16 35 D6
Peveril Cl BH24 9 H6
Phelips Rd BH21 28 A4
Phyldon Cl BH12 54 B1
Phyldon Rd BH12 54 A1
Pickard Rd BH22 24 C2
Pickering Cl BH18 36 C2
Pickford Rd BH9 40 A3
Pier App BH2 5 E5
Pig Shoot La BH23 33 H6
Pilford Heath Rd BH21 12 A6
Pilgrim Park Homes Caravan Pk BH24 19 E3
Pilgrims Cl BH25 48 D3
Pilgrims Way BH17 36 C5
Pilot Hight Rd BH11 39 F1
Pilsdon Dr BH17 37 G2
Pimpern Cl BH17 37 G2
Pine Av, Bournemouth BH6 58 C4
Pine Av, Poole BH12 39 E6
Pine Cl, Ferndown BH22 23 H1
Pine Cl, New Milton BH25 47 F7
Pine Cres BH23 45 H6
Pine Dr, Poole BH13 55 E4
Pine Dr, Ringwood BH24 15 H2
Pine End BH22 24 B5
Pine Glen Av BH22 13 G6
Pine Grange BH1 5 F3
Pine Manor Rd BH24 15 F1
Pine Mansions BH1 57 F3
Pine Park Mansions BH13 55 F3
Pine Rd, Bournemouth BH9 40 C4
Pine Rd, Wimborne BH21 28 A1
Pine Tree Cl BH21 21 F3
Pine Tree Glen BH4 55 H3
Pine Tree Walk BH17 36 B5
Pine Vale Cres BH10 40 B1
Pine View Cl, Poole BH16 34 E4
Pine View Cl, Verwood BH31 7 A2
Pine View Rd BH31 7 A2
Pine Walk BH31 7 E3
Pinebeach Ct BH13 63 H1
Pinecliff Rd BH13 63 G1
Pinecliffe Av BH6 58 C4
Pinecliffe Rd BH25 47 D7

Pineholt Cl BH24 16 B2
Pinehurst Av BH23 60 D3
Pinehurst Pk BH24 14 B6
Pinehurst Rd BH22 14 A5
Pinesprings Dr BH18 36 A2
Pinewood Av BH10 32 A5
Pinewood Cl, Bournemouth BH10 32 A5
Pinewood Cl, Christchurch BH23 47 B5
Pinewood Cl, Poole BH13 55 G6
Pinewood Cl, Upton BH16 34 C3
Pinewood Gdns BH22 23 H2
Pinewood Rd, Christchurch BH23 47 A5
Pinewood Rd, Ferndown BH22 23 H1
Pinewood Rd, Lymington SO41 50 A2
Pinewood Rd, Poole BH13 55 G6
Pinewood Rd, Ringwood BH24 15 H2
Pinewood Rd, Upton BH16 34 C3
Pipers Ash BH24 19 E4
Pipers Dr BH23 61 E1
Pippin Cl BH23 43 E4
Pitmore La SO41 64 D5
Pitmore Rd BH23 44 A3
Pitts Pl BH25 48 F4
Pitwines Cl BH15 6 C3
Plant Park Rd BH24 16 C4
Plantagenet Cres BH11 30 C5
Plantation SO41 50 B5
Plantation Ct BH17 37 E3
Plantation Dr BH23 47 B5
Plantation Rd BH17 37 E4
Plassey Cres BH10 31 G6
Playfields Dr BH12 54 D1
Pleasance Way BH25 48 A4
Plecy Cl BH22 24 A6
Plemont Cl BH12 38 D4
Pless Rd SO41 51 B3
Plover Dr SO41 51 F4
Plumer Rd BH17 36 C3
Policemans La BH16 34 B3
Pomona Cl BH22 24 A2
Pompeys La, Ferndown BH22 23 E4
Pompeys La, Ferndown BH22 23 G6
Pond Cl BH25 48 B4
Pond Head BH21 11 H1
Ponsonby Rd BH12 54 D2
Pony Dr BH16 34 F3

Poole Commercial Centre BH12 55 E2
Poole Harbour BH15 35 C8
Poole Hill BH2 4 A4
Poole La BH11 31 E6
Poole Rd, Bournemouth BH2 4 A3
Poole Rd, Bournemouth BH2,4 55 G3
Poole Rd, Poole BH12 55 G3
Poole Rd, Upton BH16 34 E3
Poole Rd, Wimborne BH21 21 E4
Popes Rd BH15 37 F6
Poplar Cl, Bransgore BH23 64 D2
Poplar Cl, Christchurch BH23 47 C7
Poplar Cl, Poole BH15 6 A4
Poplar Cl, Wimborne BH21 21 F3
Poplar Cl*, West BH15 52 D5
Poplar Cres BH24 19 E5
Poplar La BH23 64 C2
Poplar Rd BH25 48 E3
Poplar Way BH24 19 E5
Poppy Cl, Christchurch BH23 45 F5
Poppy Cl, Poole BH16 34 B3
Portarlington Cl BH4 4 A5
Portarlington Rd BH4 4 A5
Portchester Ct BH8 5 H1
Portchester Pl BH8 57 E2
Portchester Rd BH8 56 C1
Portelet Cl BH12 38 C3
Porter Rd BH17 36 C5
Porters La BH22 22 B2
Portesham Gdns BH9 41 E1
Portesham Way BH17 37 F2
Portfield Cl BH23 43 G6
Portfield Rd BH23 43 F6

Portland Pl BH2 4 D1
Portland Rd BH9 40 C4
Portman Cres BH5 58 B4
Portman Rd BH7 57 H1
Portman Ter BH5 58 B3
Portmore Cl BH18 28 D4
Portswood Dr BH10 40 C1
Post Green Rd BH16 34 A1
Post Office La,
  Poole BH15 6 C4
Post Office La,
  Ringwood BH24 16 A2
Post Office Rd BH1 4 D4
Potterne Way BH21 7 D4
Potterne Wood Cl BH31 7 F4
Potters Way BH14 54 B5
Pottery Rd BH14 54 A4
Poulner Hill BH24 19 F4
Poulner Mobile
  Home Pk BH24 19 E1
Poulner Rd BH24 19 E3
Pound Cl, Poole BH15 53 G1
Pound Cl,
  Ringwood BH24 18 C3
Pound La BH15 53 F2
Powell Rd BH14 54 A4
Powers Court Rd BH25 47 F8
Powis Cl BH15 48 C4
Preston Cl BH16 34 E3
Preston La BH23 44 A3
Preston Rd BH15 52 D1
Preston Way BH23 45 G6
Prestwood Cl BH25 49 A6
Priestley Rd BH10 39 G4
Primrose Gdns BH17 36 B3
Primrose Way,
  Christchurch BH23 45 F5
Primrose Way,
  Wimborne BH21 26 F4
Prince of Wales Rd BH4 55 G3
Princes Ct BH12 55 F3
Princes Pl BH25 48 D3
Princes Rd BH22 24 A3
Princess Av BH23 59 H2
Princess Rd,
  Bournemouth BH4 55 G3
Princess Rd,
  Poole BH12 55 F2
Pringles Cl BH23 24 B3
Pringles Dr BH22 24 B3
Priors Cl BH23 61 G1
Priors Rd BH17 36 B4
Priors Walk BH21 20 D3
Priory Cl BH23 59 H2
Priory Gdns BH22 14 C6
Priory Ind Pk BH23 45 E6
Priory Quay BH23 59 H2
Priory Rd,
  Bournemouth BH2 4 C5
Priory Rd,
  Ferndown BH22 14 C6
Priory View Pl BH9 40 D1
Priory View Rd,
  Bournemouth BH9 40 C1
Priory View Rd,
  Christchurch BH23 44 A3
Privet Rd BH9 40 B4
Promenade,
  Bournemouth BH6 59 E5
Promenade,
  Canford Cliffs BH13 63 F2
Promenade,
  Christchurch BH23 61 F2
Promenade,
  Sandbanks BH13 62 D5
Prosperous St BH15 6 B4
Prunus Cl BH22 23 G1
Prunus Dr BH22 23 G1
Puddletown Cres BH17 37 G3
Pullman Cl BH14 14 A4
Pullman Way BH24 18 D6
Purbeck Av BH15 52 A6
Purbeck Cl BH16 34 C3
Purbeck Ct BH5 58 B4
Purbeck Ct*,
  Dorset BH23 44 D5
Purbeck Dr BH31 7 C3
Purbeck Gdns BH14 53 H1
Purbeck Heights BH14 54 A2
Purbeck Rd,
  Bournemouth BH2 4 B4
Purbeck Rd,
  New Milton BH25 47 E7
Purchase Rd BH12 39 G5
Purewell BH23 60 A1
Purewell Cl BH23 60 B1
Purewell Cross Rd
  BH23 60 A1
Purewell Ct BH23 60 B1
Pussex La BH23 17 A4

Pye Cl BH23 26 F4
Pye Corner BH21 20 D4
Pye La BH21 20 D4

Quadrant Arc BH1 5 E3
Quantock Ct*,
  Hunt Rd BH23 44 D6
Quarr Ho SO41 64 B4
Quarry Cl BH21 22 A2
Quarry Dr BH21 22 A1
Quarry Rd BH21 22 A2
Quay Point BH15 6 B5
Quay Rd BH23 59 H2
Quayle Dr BH11 31 E5
Queen Anne Dr BH21 21 F3
Queen Mary Av BH9 40 C3
Queens Av BH23 59 H2
Queens Cl BH22 14 A5
Queens Ct,
  Bournemouth BH4 4 A2
Queens Ct,
  Charminster BH8 41 E4
Queens Ct,
  New Milton BH25 48 E3
Queens Gdns BH2 4 A2
Queens Gro BH25 48 E3
Queens Park Av BH8 41 E4
Queens Park Gdns BH8 41 F6
Queens Park Rd BH8 41 F6
Queens Pk South Dr
  BH8 41 F6
Queens Pk West Dr BH8 41 F5
Queens Rd,
  Bournemouth BH2 4 A3
Queens Rd,
  Christchurch BH23 60 B2
Queens Rd,
  Ferndown BH22 24 A1
Queens Rd,
  Poole BH14 54 C3
Queens Rd,
  Wimborne BH21 27 F5
Queens Way BH24 18 D4
Queensbury
  Mansions BH1 5 F4
Queensland Rd BH5 58 A3
Queensway BH25 46 F4
Queensway Av BH8 41 H4
Queenswood Dr BH22 23 H1
Quince La BH21 21 F3
Quinton Cl BH23 47 A7
Quomp BH24 18 C5

R L Stevenson Av BH4 55 G4
Rachel Cl BH12 38 B6
Radipole Rd BH17 37 H2
Raglan Gdns BH11 39 F2
Raleigh Cl,
  Christchurch BH23 60 D2
Raleigh Cl,
  New Milton BH25 48 A4
Raleigh Cl,
  Ringwood BH24 19 E3
Raleigh Rd BH23 38 D3
Ralph Rd BH21 26 F3
Ramsey St BH25 48 A4
Randalls Hill BH16 34 B2
Randolph Rd,
  Bournemouth BH1 57 G2
Randolph Rd,
  Poole BH14 54 B2
Ranelagh Rd BH23 47 A8
Raven Way BH23 60 D2
Ravens Way SO41 51 D4
Ravenscourt Rd BH6 58 C3
Ravensdale Cl BH12 54 B1
Ravenshall BH4 4 A5
Ravine Ct BH13 63 G2
Ravine Gdns BH13 63 G1
Ravine Rd,
  Bournemouth BH5 58 B4
Ravine Rd, Poole BH13 63 F1
Raymond Cl BH31 7 E2
Rayners Dr BH12 54 D1
Rebbeck Rd BH7 58 A2
Recreation Rd BH12 54 C1
Rectory Av BH21 26 E2
Rectory Rd BH15 52 D1
Red La BH21 26 C2
Red Oaks Cl BH22 23 G2
Redan Cl BH23 47 A7
Redbreast Rd BH9 40 C2
Redbreast Rd North
  BH9 40 D1
Redcliffe Cl BH23 43 H3
Redcotts La BH21 20 D3
Redcotts Rd BH21 20 C3
Redhill Av BH9 40 B3
Redhill Cl BH10 40 A2
Redhill Cres BH9 40 C1

Redhill Ct BH10 32 C6
Redhill Dr BH10 40 A2
Redhoave Rd BH17 37 F3
Redhorn Cl BH16 35 E6
Redlands BH12 55 E2
Redmans Vw BH31 7 A2
Redshank Cl BH17 36 B3
Redvers Rd BH23 44 B6
Redwood Cl BH24 18 D5
Redwood Dr BH22 13 H6
Redwood Rd BH16 34 B2
Regency Cres BH23 43 F5
Regency Pl BH24 18 C3
Regent Dr BH7 41 H5
Regent Way BH23 59 H2
Reid St BH23 43 G6
Rempstone Rd BH21 29 F1
Renault Dr BH18 36 B3
Retreat Rd BH21 21 E4
Reuben Dr BH15 35 F7
Reynard Ct BH15 53 G3
Rhiners Cl SO41 64 B4
Ribble Cl BH18 36 C2
Ribbonwood Heights
  BH14 54 B2
Ricardo Cres BH23 61 E2
Rice Gdns BH16 35 F5
Rice Ter BH16 35 F5
Richard Cl BH16 34 C2
Richmond Bridge Rd
  BH8 41 F6
Richmond Cl SO41 51 D4
Richmond Gdns BH1 4 D3
Richmond Hill BH2 4 D4
Richmond Hill Dr BH2 4 D3
Richmond Park Av BH8 41 E6
Richmond Park Cl*,
  Holdenhurst Rd BH8 57 F1
Richmond Park Cres
  BH8 41 F6
Richmond Park Rd BH8 41 E6
Richmond Rd,
  Poole BH14 54 B2
Richmond Rd,
  Wimborne BH21 21 F4
Richmond Wood Rd
  BH8 41 E6
Ridgefield Gdns BH23 45 G5
Ridgemount Gdns
  BH15 52 A3
Ridgeway,
  Broadstone BH18 28 C6
Ridgeway,
  Ferndown BH22 32 B3
Ridgeway,
  Wimborne BH21 26 F2
Ridley Rd BH9 40 C4
Ridout Cl BH10 39 G4
Riggs Gdns BH11 39 E3
Rigler Rd BH15 52 B5
Rimbury Way BH23 43 G5
Ringwood Bournemouth
  Spur Rd,
Ringwood Bournemouth
  Spur Rd BH8 42 A4
Ringwood Bournemouth
  Spur Rd,
  Ringwood BH24 16 C6
Ringwood By-Pass
  BH24 16 C2
Ringwood Rd,
  Bournemouth BH11 38 C2
Ringwood Rd,
  Bransgore BH23 64 B1
Ringwood Rd,
  Christchurch BH23 45 G1
Ringwood Rd,
  Ferndown BH22 23 G6
Ringwood Rd,
  Poole BH12,14 53 G2
Ringwood Rd,
  St Leonards BH24 15 F5
Ringwood Rd,
  Three Legged Cross
  BH21 8 A4
Ringwood Rd,
  Verwood BH31 7 C1
Ringwood Rd,
  Walkford BH23 46 A4
Ringwood Trading Est
  BH24 18 D6
Ripon Rd BH9 40 D4
Ritchie Pl BH22 14 A3
Ritchie Rd BH11 39 G1
River Cl BH21 20 D3
River Gdns SO41 51 E3
River Way BH23 42 D4
Riverdale La BH23 59 G1
Riverlea Rd BH23 59 G2
Rivermead Gdns BH23 43 E4
Riversdale Rd BH6 59 G3

Riverside BH24 18 B5
Riverside Av BH7 42 B4
Riverside La BH6 59 F3
Riverside Pk,
  Christchurch BH23 59 G2
Riverside Pk, Wimborne BH21
  21 F5
Riverside Rd,
  Bournemouth BH6 59 F3
Riverside Rd,
  Ferndown BH22 13 H4
Riviera BH1 5 H4
Riviera Ct,
  Bournemouth BH2 4 B3
Riviera Ct, Poole BH13 63 F2
Roberts Cl SO41 50 B5
Roberts La BH17 36 B5
Roberts Rd,
  Bournemouth BH7 58 A2
Roberts Rd,
  Poole BH17 36 C3
Robin Cl BH9 40 C2
Robin Cres BH25 46 F2
Robin Gdns BH23 43 F6
Robin Gro BH25 49 A5
Robins Way BH23 61 E3
Robinswood Dr BH22 24 A1
Robsall Cl BH12 38 D6
Rochester Rd BH11 39 G1
Rockbourne Gdns
  BH25 47 E7
Rockford Cl BH6 59 F4
Rockley Pk BH15 35 D7
Rockley Rd BH15 52 A5
Rodbourne Cl SO41 50 A5
Rodney Cl BH12 39 F5
Rodney Ct,
  Christchurch BH23 60 D2
Rodney Ct, Poole BH15 6 C4
Rodney Ct*,
  Whatleigh Cl BH15 53 E5
Rodney Dr BH23 60 D1
Rodway BH21 21 E4
Rodwell Cl BH10 31 H5
Roebuck Cl BH23 48 D4
Roeshot Cres BH23 44 H5
Roeshot Hill BH23 44 F4
Rolls Dr BH6 59 H4
Roman Heights BH21 28 A3
Roman Rd BH18 28 A6
Romney Rd BH10 40 B1
Rook Hill Rd BH23 61 F2
Rookcliff Way SO41 51 C3
Roosevelt Cres BH11 31 G4
Ropers La BH21 34 F3
Ropley Rd BH7 58 C1
Rosamund Av BH21 29 F2
Roscrea Cl BH6 59 G3
Roscrea Dr BH6 59 H4
Rose Cres BH15 37 G6
Rose Ct BH15 53 F3
Rose Gdns BH9 40 C2
Rosebery Cl BH31 7 F4
Rosebery Rd BH5 58 A3
Rosebud Av BH9 40 C2
Rosecrae Cl BH9 40 C2
Rosedale Cl BH23 60 C1
Rosehill Cl BH23 64 C1
Rosehill Dr BH23 64 B2
Rosemary Cl BH23 47 C7
Rosemary Gdns BH12 38 A5
Rosemary Rd BH12 38 A5
Rosemount Rd BH4 55 G5
Rosewood Gdns BH25 48 A3
Roslin Rd BH3 40 B6
Roslin Rd South BH3 40 A5
Ross Gdns BH11 30 C5
Ross Glades BH3 56 B1
Ross Rd BH24 19 F2
Rossiters Quay BH23 60 A2
Rossley Cl BH23 45 H4
Rossmore Par BH12 38 B4
Rossmore Rd BH12 38 B4
Rotary Cl BH21 21 H1
Rothbury Pk BH25 48 D4
Rotherfield Rd,
  Bournemouth BH5 58 B4
Rotherfield Rd,
  Christchurch BH23 47 B6
Rothesay Dr BH23 45 H6
Rothesay Rd BH4 55 H1
Rotterdam Dr BH23 60 A1
Roumelia La BH5 57 G3
Roundhaye Rd BH11 31 E5
Roundways BH11 39 E2
Rowan Cl,
  Christchurch BH23 45 G5
Rowan Cl,
  Lymington SO41 64 B6

Rowan Cl,
  Ringwood BH24 15 F3
Rowan Dr,
  Christchurch BH23 45 G5
Rowan Dr, Poole BH17 36 A4
Rowan Dr,
  Verwood BH31 7 G2
Rowbarrow Cl BH17 37 G2
Rowe Gdns BH12 39 E6
Rowena Rd BH6 59 F3
Rowland Av BH15 53 F1
Rowlands Hill BH21 21 E4
Rownhams Rd BH8 41 F2
Royal Arc BH1 57 G2
Royal Mews BH21 21 E4
Royal Oak Rd BH10 31 H5
Royster Cl BH17 37 E4
Royston Dr BH21 21 E3
Royston Pl BH25 49 C7
Rozel Manor BH13 55 G4
Rozelle Rd BH14 54 B2
Rubens Cl BH25 48 C3
Rufford Gdns BH6 59 E3
Rugby Rd BH17 37 F3
Runnymede Av BH11 30 C4
Runton Rd BH12 55 E2
Rushall La BH21 26 C4
Rushcombe Way BH21 26 F6
Rushford Warren BH23 60 C3
Rushmere Rd BH6 58 C1
Rushton Cres BH3 56 C1
Ruskin Av BH9 40 D1
Russel Rd BH10 31 H4
Russell Cotes Rd BH1 5 F5
Russell Cl BH23 48 B4
Russell Dr BH23 60 B1
Russell Gdns,
  Poole BH16 35 D6
Russell Gdns,
  Ringwood BH24 16 B2
Russet Cl BH22 23 H2
Rutland Rd,
  Bournemouth BH9 40 D4
Rutland Rd,
  Christchurch BH23 43 F4
Ryall Rd BH17 37 E3
Ryan Cl BH22 23 H1
Ryan Gdns,
  Bournemouth BH11 31 G5
Ryan Gdns,
  Ferndown BH22 23 H1
Rydal Cl BH23 42 D2
Ryecroft Av BH11 30 D5

Saddle BH23 22 B2
Saffron Dr BH23 45 E6
Saffron Way BH11 38 C1
St Albans Av BH8 41 E3
St Albans Cres BH8 41 E3
St Albans Rd BH8 41 E3
St Aldhelms Cl BH13 55 E3
St Aldhelms Rd BH13 55 E3
St Andrews Rd BH18 28 C5
St Annes Av BH6 59 E3
St Annes Rd BH16 34 D2
St Anns Ct*,
  Palmerston Mews
  BH1 57 G2
St Anthonys Rd BH2 56 B2
St Aubyns Ct BH15 6 B4
St Aubyns La BH24 19 G2
St Augustins Rd BH2 56 B1
St Brelades Av BH12 38 C3
St Catherines BH21 21 E4
St Catherines Path BH6 59 E5
St Catherines Rd BH6 59 E4
St Catherines Way
  BH23 42 D3
St Clair Rd BH13 63 F2
St Cleeve Way BH22 23 H6
St Clements Gdns BH1 57 F2
St Clements La BH15 6 B5
St Clements Rd,
  Bournemouth BH1 57 F2
St Clements Rd,
  Poole BH15 38 A6
St Davids Ct*,
  Palmerston Mews BH1 57 G2
St Davids Rd BH16 34 D2
St Denys*,
  Station Rd BH25 49 C5
St Georges Av,
  Bournemouth BH8 41 F5
St Georges Av,
  Poole BH12 38 A4
St Georges Cl,
  Bournemouth BH8 41 F5
St Georges Cl,
  Bransgore BH23 64 C2

St Georges Cl, Christchurch BH23 45 G6
St Georges Ct*, Palmerston Mews BH157 G2
St Georges Dr, Bournemouth BH11 38 D1
St Georges Dr, Ferndown BH22 23 G4
St Helier Rd BH12 38 C3
St Ives End La BH24 16 A3
St Ives Gdns BH2 56 C2
St Ives Pk BH24 16 A2
St Ives Wood BH24 16 B2
St James Cl BH15 6 A4
St James Rd, Ferndown BH22 23 F2
St James Rd, Lymington SO41 64 C5
St James Sq BH5 58 A3
St Johns Cl BH21 21 E4
St Johns Ct*, Palmerston Mews BH1 57 G2
St Johns Gdns BH9 40 C3
St Johns Hill BH21 21 E3
St Johns Mews BH9 40 C2
St Johns Rd, Bournemouth BH5 57 G3
St Johns Rd, Christchurch BH23 59 F1
St Johns Rd, Poole BH15 6 D1
St Just Cl BH22 23 G5
St Ledgers Pl BH8 41 G6
St Ledgers Rd BH8 41 F6
St Leonards Rd BH 56 D1
St Leonards Way BH24 15 G2
St Lukes Rd BH3 40 B5
St Maradox La BH9 40 D3
St Margarets BH2 4 D1
St Margarets Almshouses BH21 20 C3
St Margarets Av BH23 59 G2
St Margarets Cl BH21 20 C3
St Margarets Hill BH21 20 C2
St Margarets Rd, Bournemouth BH10 39 G3
St Margarets Rd, Poole BH15 6 D1
St Marks Rd BH11 39 G2
St Martins Rd BH6 34 C3
St Mary Gro SO41 50 C3
St Marys Cl BH23 64 C6
St Marys Ct BH6 59 E4
St Marys Mews BH22 24 A4
St Marys Rd, Ferndown BH22 23 H3
St Marys Rd, Poole BH15 6 D2
St Marys Rd, Springbourne BH1 57 F1
St Merrins Cl BH10 39 H1
St Michaels Cl, Poole BH15 52 A4
St Michaels Cl, Verwood BH31 7 C3
St Michaels Mews BH2 4 B4
St Michaels Pl BH2 4 B4
St Michaels Rd, Bournemouth BH2 4 B4
St Michaels Rd, Verwood BH31 7 C3
St Osmunds Rd BH14 54 B3
St Pauls La BH8 5 G2
St Pauls Pl BH8 5 G2
St Pauls Rd BH8 5 G1
St Peters Cres BH1 5 E4
St Peters Ct BH1 5 E3
St Peters Rd, Bournemouth BH1 5 E4
St Peters Rd, Poole BH14 53 H2
St Peters Walk BH1 4 D4
St Saviours Cl BH7 42 C6
St Stephens Ct BH2 4 B4
St Stephens La BH31 7 D2
St Stephens Rd BH2 4 C3
St Stephens Way BH2 4 D3
St Swithuns Rd BH1 5 H2
St Swithuns Rd South BH1 5 H2
StThomas Cl BH10 40 A2
St Valerie Rd BH2 4 D1
St Winifreds Rd BH2 56 B2
Saints Cl BH21 7 H2
Salerno Pl BH15 35 F8
Salisbury Rd, Bournemouth BH1 57 G2
Salisbury Rd, Christchurch BH23 44 A2

Salisbury Rd, Poole BH14 54 B2
Salisbury Rd, Ringwood BH24 18 C4
Salter Rd BH13 62 C5
Salterns Ct BH14 54 A6
Salterns Rd BH14 54 A4
Salterns Way BH14 62 C1
Saltings Rd BH16 34 D4
Samantha Cl BH10 40 A1
Samples Way BH17 37 G5
Samson Rd BH15 35 F7
Samsons Cotts BH21 22 D4
San Remo Towers BH5 57 G3
Sancreed Rd BH12 54 C6
Sandbanks Bsns Centre BH13 62 B6
Sandbanks Rd BH14 53 G3
Sandbourne Rd, Bournemouth BH4 55 G6
Sandbourne Rd, Poole BH15 53 F2
Sandecotes Rd BH14 54 B3
Sanderlings BH24 19 E6
Sandford Cl BH9 41 F1
Sandford Way BH18 36 B2
Sandhills BH17 37 F2
Sandhurst Dr BH21 8 C5
Sandmartin Cl BH25 49 A8
Sandown Rd BH23 60 C1
Sandpiper Cl BH17 36 B3
Sandpit La BH15 6 D2
Sandringham Cl BH9 32 D6
Sandringham Ct BH8 41 E6
Sandringham Gdns BH9 32 D6
Sandringham Rd BH14 53 H6
Sandy Cl BH21 11 H6
Sandy La, Bournemouth BH7 58 B2
Sandy La, Christchurch BH23 43 E3
Sandy La, Poole BH14 34 C3
Sandy La, Ringwood BH24 15 H2
Sandy La,Three Legged Cross BH21 8 A2
Sandy La, Verwood BH31 7 D2
Sandy La, Wimborne BH21 12 A6
Sandy Mead Rd BH8 41 H4
Sandy Plot BH23 44 A5
Sandy Way BH10 40 B1
Sandyhurst Cl BH17 37 E4
Sarah Cl BH7 42 B6
Sarah Sands Cl BH23 44 B6
Sark Rd BH12 38 C5
Sarum Av BH22 14 A2
Sarum Ct BH14 54 B3
Sarum St BH15 6 B5
Saulfland Dr BH23 45 G6
Saulfland Pl BH23 45 G5
Saxon Centre BH23 59 H1
Saxon King Gdns BH6 59 H4
Saxon Sq BH23 59 H1
Saxonbury Rd BH6 59 E2
Saxonford Rd BH23 61 F1
Saxonhurst Cl BH10 32 B5
Saxonhurst Gdns BH10 32 B6
Saxonhurst Rd BH10 32 B6
Scarf Rd BH17 37 G5
School Cl BH31 7 D2
School La, Bournemouth BH11 31 G5
School La, Lymington SO41 51 E2
School La, Poole BH15 53 E2
School La, Ringwood BH24 18 C4
School La, St Ives BH24 16 A2
School La, Three Legged Cross BH21 8 C5
School La, Wimborne BH21 20 D3
Scott Cl BH12 39 E4
Scott Rd BH12 39 E4
Scotter Rd BH7 58 B2
Scotts Grn BH17 44 D6
Scotts Hills La BH23 60 A1
Sea Rd, Boscombe BH5 57 G4
Sea Rd, Lymington SO41 51 E4
Sea Rd, New Milton BH25 47 F6
Sea Rd, Southbourne BH6 59 F5

Sea View Rd, New Milton BH25 47 E7
Sea View Rd, Poole BH12 54 A1
Sea View Rd, Upton BH16 34 C3
Sea Vixen Ind Est BH23 44 D6
Seabank Cl BH16 34 C3
Seabourne Pl BH5 58 B3
Seabourne Rd BH5 58 B2
Seacliff Ct BH6 58 D4
Seacombe Rd BH13 62 C6
Seacroft Av BH25 47 F7
Seafield Cl BH25 49 A7
Seafield Dr BH6 59 E2
Seafield Rd, Bournemouth BH6 58 D4
Seafield Rd, Christchurch BH23 61 F1
Seafield Rd, New Milton BH25 47 F7
Seagrim Rd BH8 41 F2
Seagull Rd BH8 41 F3
Seamoor La BH4 55 G3
Seamoor Rd BH4 55 G3
Seaton Cl BH23 47 C6
Seaton Rd BH23 47 C6
Seatown Cl BH17 37 H3
Seaview Rd BH23 47 D5
Seaward Av, Bournemouth BH6 58 C4
Seaward Av, New Milton BH25 47 F7
Seaway BH25 49 D7
Seaway Av BH23 61 F1
Seawinds SO41 51 B3
Second Marine Av BH25 49 B8
Sedgley Rd BH9 40 B5
Selby Cl BH18 36 C1
Seldown BH15 6 D3
Seldown Bri BH15 6 D4
Seldown La BH15 6 D3
Seldown Rd BH15 6 D3
Selfridge Av BH6 59 H4
Selfridge Cl BH6 59 H4
Seliot Cl BH15 53 F2
Selkirk Cl BH21 29 G1
Sellwood Way BH25 47 E7
Selworthy Cl BH14 54 A4
Serpentine La South BH15 53 E4
Serpentine Rd BH15 6 C2
Serpentine Rd South BH15 6 C3
Set Thorns Rd SO41 64 C5
Setley Gdns BH8 41 G2
Sevenoaks Dr BH7 42 A6
Severn Rd BH22 24 D3
Seymour Rd BH24 18 D3
Shackleton Sq BH23 64 C1
Shaftesbury Cl BH22 14 C5
Shaftesbury Rd, Bournemouth BH8 41 F6
Shaftesbury Rd, Ferndown BH22 14 B5
Shaftesbury Rd, Poole BH15 6 D1
Shakespeare Rd, Bournemouth BH6 58 D1
Shakespeare Rd, Wimborne BH21 20 D2
Shapland Av BH11 30 D6
Shapwick Rd BH15 52 C6
Shard Cl BH31 7 D2
Sharlands Cl BH18 36 D1
Sharp Rd BH12 54 D6
Sharvells Rd SO41 51 C3
Shaves Cl BH25 48 C2
Shaw Rd BH24 19 F2
Shawford Gdns BH8 41 F2
Shawford Rd BH8 41 F2
Shears Brook Cl BH23 64 C1
Shelbourne Rd BH8 40 D6
Sheldrake Gdns SO41 50 C2
Sheldrake Rd BH23 61 E2
Shelley Cl, Bournemouth BH1 57 G2
Shelley Cl, Christchurch BH23 45 G6
Shelley Cl, Ringwood BH24 15 G1
Shelley Dr BH22 23 H3
Shelley Gdns BH1 57 G1
Shelley Hill BH23 45 F6
Shelley Rd, Bournemouth BH1 57 G2
Shelley Rd, Poole BH12 54 C2

Shelley Rd East BH7 57 H2
Shelley Way SO41 51 E3
Shelton Rd BH6 58 C2
Shenstone Ct BH25 49 B5
Shepherd Cl BH23 47 A6
Shepherds Way, Bournemouth BH7 42 A6
Shepherds Way, Lymington SO41 50 A5
Sheppards Fld BH21 20 D2
Sherborn Cres BH17 37 G3
Sherborne Dr BH22 24 A5
Sherfield Cl BH8 41 F2
Sheringham Rd BH12 55 E1
Sherrin Cl BH15 53 E2
Sherwood Av, Ferndown BH22 23 H5
Sherwood Av, Poole BH14 53 H4
Sherwood Cl BH23 43 F6
Sherwood Dr BH31 7 E2
Shetland Vw BH31 7 D2
Shillingstone Dr BH9 33 E6
Shillito Rd BH12 54 C2
Shinglebank Dr SO41 51 D3
Shipstal Cl BH16 35 E6
Shires Copse BH6 59 F4
Shires Mead BH31 7 D2
Shirley Cl, Christchurch BH23 64 C1
Shirley Cl, Ferndown BH22 14 B4
Shirley Rd, Bournemouth BH9 40 D4
Shirley Rd, Poole BH12 54 A1
Shirley Rd, Upton BH16 34 D3
Shore Av BH16 34 D4
Shore Cl, Lymington SO41 51 E4
Shore Cl, Poole BH16 34 E4
Shore Gdns BH16 34 D4
Shore La BH16 34 E4
Shore Rd BH14 62 D2
Shorefield Cres SO41 51 C2
Shorefield Rd SO41 51 A1
Shorefield Way SO41 51 C2
Short Cl BH12 39 F4
Shorts Cl BH23 44 A4
Shottsford Rd BH15 53 E1
Sidney Gdns BH9 33 E6
Sidney Smith Ct*, Walditch Gdns BH17 37 F2
Silchester Cl BH2 4 D1
Silver Bsns Pk BH23 55 F2
Silver St, Christchurch BH23 59 H2
Silver St, Lymington SO41 50 A1
Silver Way BH23 45 H6
Silverdale BH25 49 C7
Silverdale Cl BH18 36 A1
Silverwood Cl BH21 21 F6
Simmonds Cl BH15 53 E1
Singleton Dr BH10 39 H3
Siskin Cl BH22 23 G1
Sixpenny Cl BH12 39 E5
Skinner St BH15 6 B4
Skipton Cl BH18 36 B3
Sky End La SO41 50 C3
Slade Cl SO41 50 B2
Slades Farm Rd BH10 39 H3
Sleepbrook Cl BH31 7 B2
Sleight La BH21 26 E2
Slepe Cres BH12 39 E5
Slinn Rd BH23 44 B6
Slip Way BH15 6 B3
Slough La BH16 34 A4
Smithfield Pl BH9 40 B4
Smithson Cl BH12 39 G5
Smithy La BH25 48 A1
Smugglers La BH21 11 E5
Smugglers La North BH23 45 G5
Smugglers La South BH23 45 H5
Smugglers Reach BH23 60 D3
Smugglers Wood Rd BH23 45 G5
Snails La BH24 18 C1
Snowdon Rd BH4 55 G3
Snowdrop Gdns BH23 45 E5
Snowy Cl BH12 39 F4
Soberton Rd BH8 41 G6
Solent Cl SO41 51 C3
Solent Dr BH25 49 B7
Solent Pines SO41 51 B3

Solent Prom BH6 59 F5
Solent Rd, Bournemouth BH6 59 G5
Solent Rd, Christchurch BH23 47 C5
Solent Rd, Naish Est BH25 47 E7
Solent Vw BH6 59 G5
Solent Way SO41 51 F3
Solly Cl BH12 38 D5
Solomon Way BH15 35 F7
Somerby Rd BH15 37 F6
Somerford Av BH23 45 E6
Somerford Bsns Pk BH23 44 D6
Somerford Rd BH23 60 B1
Somerford Way BH23 60 C1
Somerley Rd BH9 40 C5
Somerley Vw BH24 18 C3
Somerset Rd, Bournemouth BH7 58 A2
Somerset Rd, Christchurch BH23 43 E6
Somerton Cl BH25 48 E4
Somerville Ct*, Marryat Rd BH25 48 A4
Somerville Rd, Bournemouth BH2 4 A4
Somerville Rd, Ringwood BH24 19 E3
Sonning Way BH8 41 E3
Sopers La, Christchurch BH23 59 G2
Sopers La, Poole BH17 36 B3
Sopley Cl BH23 47 E7
Sopwith Cl BH23 61 E1
Sopwith Cres BH21 29 F1
Sorrel Gdns BH18 36 B2
Sorrell Cl BH23 45 E6
Sorrell Way BH23 45 E5
South Av BH25 49 C5
South Cliff Rd BH2 4 D5
South Haven Cl BH16 35 D6
South Kinson Dr BH11 31 F6
South Lawns Walk BH25 49 A6
South Park Rd BH12 39 F5
South Rd, Bournemouth BH1 5 E5
South Rd, Poole BH15 6 C4
South Rd, Springbourne BH1 57 G1
South Rd, Wimborne BH21 26 F4
South Sway La SO41 64 C6
South View Pl BH2 4 B4
South View Rd BH23 59 G2
South Vw BH2 4 D1
South Western Cres BH14 54 A4
Southampton Rd BH24 18 C4
Southbourne Coast Rd BH6 59 E5
Southbourne Gro BH6 58 B3
Southbourne La Central BH6 58 C3
Southbourne La East BH6 58 C3
Southbourne La West BH6 58 C3
Southbourne Overcliff Dr BH6 58 C5
Southbourne Prom BH6 58 C5
Southbourne Rd BH6 58 B2
Southbourne Sands BH6 58 D4
Southbrook Cl BH17 37 H3
Southcliffe Rd, Christchurch BH23 61 F1
Southcliffe Rd, New Milton BH25 47 H3
Southcote Rd BH1 5 H2
Southdown Ct*, Dorset Rd BH23 44 C5
Southdown Way BH22 14 B5
Southern Av BH22 14 C5
Southern La BH25 49 A6
Southern Oaks BH25 49 A6
Southern Rd BH6 58 C4
Southernhay Rd BH31 7 F2
Southey Rd BH23 44 C6
Southfield BH24 18 C6
Southfield Mews BH24 18 C6
Southill Av BH12 38 B6
Southill Gdns BH9 40 D4
Southill Rd, Bournemouth BH9 40 D4
Southill Rd, Poole BH12 38 C6

Southlands Av, Bournemouth BH6 59 F4
Southlands Av, Wimborne BH21 26 F4
Southlands Ct BH18 36 C1
Southlea Av BH6 59 E3
Southville Rd BH6 58 B3
Southwick Pl BH6 58 C1
Southwick Rd BH6 58 C2
Southwood Av, Bournemouth BH6 58 C4
Southwood Av, Christchurch BH23 47 C6
Southwood Cl, Christchurch BH23 47 B5
Southwood Cl, Ferndown BH22 23 H3
Sovereign Bsns Pk BH15 36 D6
Sovereign Centre BH1 57 H2
Sovereign Cl BH7 41 H5
Sparkford Cl BH7 42 B6
Speedwell Dr BH23 45 E5
Spencer Rd, Bournemouth BH1 57 E2
Spencer Rd, New Milton BH25 48 C4
Spencer Rd, Poole BH13 54 D6
Spetisbury Cl BH9 41 E1
Spicer La BH11 30 D6
Spinacre BH21 49 C7
Spindle Cl BH18 36 A2
Spindlewood Cl BH25 49 B6
Spinners BH22 14 A5
Spinney Cl BH24 15 G2
Spinney Way BH25 48 C1
Spinneys La BH22 24 A4
Spittlefields BH24 19 E4
Spring Cl BH31 7 C3
Spring Gdns BH12 54 C1
Spring Hill Cotts BH21 10 C3
Spring La BH25 49 E5
Spring Rd BH1 57 E2
Springbank Rd BH7 42 A6
Springdale Av BH18 28 B6
Springdale Gro BH21 27 F6
Springdale Rd, Broadstone BH18 28 A6
Springdale Rd, Wimborne BH21 27 E6
Springfield Av, Bournemouth BH6 59 F3
Springfield Av, Christchurch BH23 42 D4
Springfield Cl BH31 7 C3
Springfield Cres BH14 54 A2
Springfield Gdns BH25 48 E4
Springfield Rd, Poole BH14 54 A1
Springfield Rd, Verwood BH31 7 B3
Springfields BH21 11 G2
Springvale Av BH7 42 A6
Springwater Cl BH11 39 F1
Springwater Dr BH22 60 A2
Springwater Rd BH11 39 F1
Spruce Cl BH17 36 A3
Spur Cl BH21 22 B2
Spur Hill Av BH14 54 C3
Spur Rd BH14 54 C3
Spurgeon Rd BH7 58 B2
Square Cl BH21 23 E5
Squirrel Walk BH31 7 C3
Squirrels Cl BH23 42 D4
Stacey Cl BH12 38 C6
Stacey Gdns BH8 41 H2
Stadium Way BH15 6 C2
Stafford Rd BH1 5 F3
Stag Bsns Pk BH24 18 C6
Stag Cl BH25 48 A3
Stagswood BH31 7 A2
Stalbridge Dr BH22 23 H5
Stalbridge Rd BH17 36 C5
Stalham Rd BH12 55 E1
Stallards La BH24 18 B4
Stamford Rd BH6 58 C3
Stanfield Cl BH12 38 C5
Stanfield Rd, Bournemouth BH9 40 B5
Stanfield Rd, Ferndown BH22 23 G2
Stanfield Rd, Poole BH12 38 C5
Stanford Rise SO41 64 B5
Stanley Cl BH31 7 D3
Stanley Ct BH15 37 E6

Stanley Green Cres BH15 52 D2
Stanley Green Rd BH15 52 D1
Stanley Grn Ind Est BH15 52 D2
Stanley Pearce Ho BH17 37 E3
Stanley Rd, Bournemouth BH1 57 E2
Stanley Rd, Christchurch BH23 47 B7
Stanley Rd, Poole BH15 6 C5
Stannington Cl BH21 49 C5
Stanpit BH23 60 B1
Stanton Rd BH10 39 H2
Stapehill Cres BH21 22 B3
Stapehill Rd BH21 23 E3
Staple Close La BH15 37 E6
Staplecross La BH23 44 B5
Stapleford Av BH22 24 B2
Star La BH24 18 B4
Starlight Farm Cl BH31 7 D2
Station App BH18 28 C6
Station Rd, Christchurch BH23 59 G1
Station Rd, Ferndown BH22 14 A2
Station Rd, Hamworthy BH15 52 C6
Station Rd, Hinton BH23 45 H3
Station Rd, Lymington SO41 64 B5
Station Rd, New Milton BH25 48 B4
Station Rd, Parkstone BH14 54 A3
Station Rd, Verwood BH31 7 A1
Station Rd, Wimborne BH21 21 E5
Station Ter BH21 21 E4
Staunton BH2 4 D5
Stedman Rd BH5 58 B3
Steepdene BH14 54 A3
Steeple Cl BH17 37 F2
Steepleton Rd BH18 37 E2
Stella Ct BH23 47 C7
Stem La BH25 46 F2
Stenhurst Rd BH15 53 F1
Stephen Langton Dr BH11 30 D5
Stephens Walk*, Kings Arms La BH24 18 B5
Sterte Av BH15 6 A1
Sterte Av West BH15 6 A1
Sterte Cl BH15 6 B1
Sterte Ct BH15 6 B1
Sterte Esp BH15 52 D3
Sterte Esplanade BH15 6 B1
Sterte Ind Est BH15 6 B1
Sterte Rd BH15 6 B1
Stevenson Cl BH23 21 E4
Stevenson Cres BH14 54 D3
Stevenson Rd BH6 59 F5
Stewart Cl BH8 57 E1
Stewart Rd BH8 56 D1
Stewarts Way BH22 24 B1
Stibbs Way BH23 64 D1
Stillmore Rd BH11 38 C1
Stinsford Cl BH9 33 E6
Stinsford Rd BH17 37 E3
Stirling Cl BH25 48 D4
Stirling Rd BH3 40 A5
Stirling Way BH23 61 E1
Stirrup Cl, Poole BH16 34 F3
Stirrup Cl, Wimborne BH21 22 B2
Stoborough Dr BH18 36 B2
Stockbridge Cl BH17 38 A2
Stoke Wood Rd BH3 40 C6
Stokes Av BH15 53 E2
Stone Gdns BH8 42 A3
Stone La BH21 20 C2
Stone La Ind Est BH21 20 C2
Stonechat Cl BH22 13 G6
Stonechat Ct BH23 60 C1
Stonecrop Cl BH18 36 A2
Stoneleigh Av SO41 50 A1
Stony La BH23 43 H2
Stony La South BH23 60 A1
Stopples La SO41 50 A1
Story La BH18 28 C6
Stour Cl BH21 22 C4
Stour Pk BH10 32 B4
Stour Rd, Bournemouth BH8 41 F6

Stour Rd, Christchurch BH23 59 F3
Stour View Gdns BH21 28 A1
Stour Walk BH8 33 G6
Stour Way BH23 42 D4
Stourbank Rd BH23 59 G2
Stourcliffe Av BH6 58 C4
Stourcroft Dr BH23 42 D4
Stourfield Rd BH5 58 C4
Stourpaine Rd BH17 37 F2
Stourvale Av BH23 42 D5
Stourvale Pl BH5 58 B2
Stourvale Rd BH5,6 58 B2
Stourwood Av BH6 58 C4
Stourwood Rd BH6 58 D4
Stouts La BH23 64 C2
Strand St BH15 6 B5
Stratfield Pl BH25 48 A4
Strathmore Dr BH31 7 D2
Strathmore Rd BH9 32 C6
Stratton Rd BH9 41 E1
Strete Mount BH23 60 B1
Stretton Ct BH14 54 A3
Strides La BH24 18 B4
Strode Gdns BH24 16 B2
Stroud Cl BH21 21 H2
Stroud Gdns BH23 60 C1
Stroud La BH23 60 C1
Stroud Park Av BH23 60 C1
Strouden Av BH8 42 A4
Strouden Rd BH9 40 C4
Struan Cl BH24 9 H6
Struan Ct BH24 16 A1
Struan Dr BH24 16 A1
Struan Gdns BH24 16 A1
Stuart Cl BH11 34 D2
Stuart Rd BH23 47 C7
Studland Dr SO41 51 C3
Studland Rd BH4 55 G5
Studley Cl BH23 47 D6
Studley Ct BH25 47 E7
Sturminster Rd BH9 32 D6
Sturt La BH8 42 B2
Suffolk Av BH23 43 F4
Suffolk Cl BH21 22 B2
Suffolk Rd BH2 4 A,B3
Suffolk Rd South BH2 4 A3
Summer Flds BH31 7 B4
Summercroft Way BH22 14 B4
Summerfield Cl, Christchurch BH23 44 A3
Summerfield Cl, Wimborne BH21 22 A4
Summerfields BH7 41 H5
Summers Av BH11 31 G5
Summers La BH21 22 A4
Summertrees Ct BH25 48 E3
Sunbury Cl BH11 31 F5
Sunbury Ct BH2 4 C3
Sunderland Dr BH23 61 F1
Sundew Cl, Christchurch BH23 45 F5
Sundew Cl, New Milton BH25 48 F3
Sunningdale BH6 36 A3
Sunningdale Cres BH10 39 H1
Sunningdale Gdns BH18 36 C5
Sunny Hill Ct BH12 54 C1
Sunny Hill Rd BH12 54 C1
Sunnybank Dr BH21 22 A2
Sunnybank Rd BH21 22 A3
Sunnybank Way BH21 22 A2
Sunnyfield Rd BH25 49 B7
Sunnyhill Rd BH6 58 B3
Sunnylands Av BH6 59 F4
Sunnymoor Rd BH11 39 F4
Sunnyside Rd BH12 38 C6
Sunnyside Residential Caravan Pk BH24 16 C2
Sunridge Cl BH12 39 F6
Sunset Lodge BH13 55 F4
Surrey Cl BH23 43 F4
Surrey Gdns BH4 55 H3
Surrey Rd, Bournemouth BH2 4 A2
Surrey Rd, Poole BH4,12 55 F2
Surrey Rd South BH4 55 H3
Sussex Cl BH9 33 E6
Sutherland Av BH18 28 A3
Sutton Cl BH17 38 A3
Sutton Rd BH9 40 D4
Swallow Cl BH17 36 A4
Swallow Dr SO41 51 F4
Swallow Way BH21 21 H1
Swan Grn BH23 59 F2
Swan Mead BH24 19 F6

Swanmore Cl BH7 58 C1
Swanmore Rd BH7 58 B1
Swansbury Dr BH8 42 B3
Sway Gdns BH8 41 G2
Sway Pk Ind Est SO41 64 B6
Sway Rd BH25 48 B1
Swift Cl BH17 36 B5
Swordfish Dr BH23 61 E1
Sycamore Cl, Christchurch BH23 42 D6
Sycamore Cl, Lymington SO41 51 D2
Sycamore Cl BH17 36 A4
Sycamore Ct BH24 19 E1
Sycamore Pl BH21 22 C3
Sycamore Rd SO41 50 A1
Sydling Cl BH17 38 A2
Sydney Rd, Broadstone BH18 36 C2
Sydney Rd, Christchurch BH23 43 E5
Sylmor Gdns BH9 40 D3
Sylvan Cl, Lymington SO41 50 C3
Sylvan Cl, Ringwood BH24 15 G2
Sylvan Rd BH12 54 A1
Symes Rd BH15 52 A3

Tadden Walk BH18 36 B2
Tait Cl BH17 37 G5
Talbot Av BH3 40 A5
Talbot Ct BH9 40 B4
Talbot Dr, Christchurch BH23 47 A5
Talbot Dr, Poole BH12 39 F5
Talbot Hill Rd BH9 40 A5
Talbot Mdws BH12 39 G4
Talbot Mews BH10 39 F4
Talbot Rd BH9 40 A5
Talbot Rise BH10 39 H3
Talbot Vw BH10 40 A3
Tamar Cl BH23 24 D3
Tamworth Rd BH7 57 H1
Tan Howse Cl BH7 42 B5
Tangmere Cl BH23 61 E1
Tangmere Pl BH17 37 F5
Tapper Ct BH21 21 F5
Tarn Dr BH17 36 B4
Tarrant Cl BH17 37 F2
Tarrant Rd BH9 41 E1
Tasman Cl BH23 43 F5
Tatnam Cres BH15 6 D1
Tatnam La BH15 6 C1
Tatnam Rd BH15 53 E2
Taverner Cl BH15 6 D4
Taylor Dr BH8 33 F6
Taylor Way BH31 7 D2
Taylors Bldgs BH15 6 C5
Teak Cl BH13 55 G6
Teasel Way BH22 14 B5
Tebourba Cotts SO41 64 C6
Technology Rd BH17 36 C4
Tedder Cl BH11 39 G1
Tedder Gdns BH11 39 G1
Tedder Rd BH11 39 G1
Telford Rd BH21 13 F6
Temple Mews BH1 57 F1
Templer Ct BH11 39 E3
Tennyson Rd, Bournemouth BH9 40 C2
Tennyson Rd, Poole BH14 53 H4
Tennyson Rd, Wimborne BH21 20 D2
Tensing Rd BH23 44 B6
Terence Av BH17 37 E3
Terence Rd BH21 27 E5
Tern Ct BH6 58 D1
Terrace Mount BH2 4 C4
Terrace Rd BH2 4 C4
Terrington Av BH23 45 H4
Thames Alley BH15 6 B5
Thames Cl BH22 24 D2
Thames Mews BH15 6 A5
Thames St BH15 6 A5
The Acorns BH1 22 A4
The Albany BH1 57 E4
The Alpha Centre BH17 36 C6
The Arcade BH1 4 D4
The Avenue, Bournemouth BH9 40 C2
The Avenue, Ferndown BH22 14 A3
The Avenue, Poole BH13 55 F6

The Avenue Shopping Centre BH2 4 C4
The Beeches BH7 42 A6
The Boltons SO41 51 D4
The Bridges BH24 18 B5
The Broads BH21 20 B2
The Broadway BH10 32 A5
The Bucklers SO41 51 B2
The Buttery BH23 60 B1
The Cedars BH4 55 H3
The Chantry BH1 5 F3
The Charltons BH23 56 C1
The Chase, Ringwood BH24 16 D2
The Chase, Verwood BH31 7 E2
The Cheviots BH14 54 C4
The Circle, Bournemouth BH9 40 C1
The Circle, Poole BH13 63 F2
The Cloisters BH21 19 F5
The Close, Avon Castle BH24 16 D3
The Close, Broadstone BH18 36 A1
The Close, Lymington SO41 64 B5
The Close, New Milton BH25 49 C7
The Close, Ringwood BH24 18 C4
The Close, St Ives BH24 16 A3
The Clovers BH12 39 F4
The Coppice BH24 61 E2
The Crescent, Bournemouth BH1 57 G2
The Crescent, New Milton BH25 47 E7
The Crossways BH16 34 E3
The Cul de Sac BH25 47 E7
The Curlews BH31 7 D3
The Deans BH1 5 E1
The Dell BH25 47 D7
The Drive BH12 54 C1
The Fairway BH25 49 C7
The Fallows BH25 48 D2
The Firs BH1 5 F3
The Forelle Centre BH31 7 F4
The Forestside BH31 7 F3
The Furlong BH24 18 B4
The Glade BH24 15 G1
The Glen BH13 63 F1
The Grange SO41 50 B5
The Green SO41 51 E3
The Grove, Bournemouth BH9 40 B2
The Grove, Christchurch BH23 42 D5
The Grove, Ferndown BH22 23 H4
The Grove, Verwood BH31 7 C3
The Hampshire Centre BH8 41 G2
The Hawthorns BH23 60 C1
The Horseshoe BH13 62 C5
The Hurdles BH23 43 E6
The Hyde BH25 48 A3
The Kingfishers BH31 7 D3
The Kiosks BH15 6 B5
The Lane BH8 57 F1
The Lanes BH25 48 B2
The Lansdowne BH1 5 G3
The Laurels BH22 23 H1
The Lawns BH23 47 C7
The Lea BH31 7 D3
The Lindens BH23 44 B3
The Lydgate SO41 51 B3
The Maitlands BH4 4 A5
The Mallows BH25 48 E3
The Marina BH5 57 G4
The Martells BH25 49 C7
The Meadow BH25 47 D7
The Meadway BH23 45 G4
The Meridians BH23 59 F2
The Mews, Bournemouth BH4 4 B4
The Mews, Verwood BH31 7 D4
The Mount BH24 19 F4
The Oaks BH31 7 B1
The Oasis BH13 55 F3
The Old Rope Walk BH15 52 B5
The Orchard, Bournemouth BH11 30 C4
The Orchard, Christchurch BH23 64 D2

The Orchard, Lymington SO41 51 E3
The Paddocks BH10 32 A6
The Parade, Ashley BH25 48 E4
The Parade, Bournemouth BH6 59 E4
The Parade, New Milton BH25 49 A6
The Parade, Wimborne BH21 27 F5
The Park BH25 47 D7
The Pines BH13 55 F5
The Point BH5 57 G4
The Quay BH15 6 A5
The Runway BH23 45 F6
The Seed Warehouse BH15 6 B5
The Spinney BH24 9 H6
The Square, Bournemouth BH2 4 D4
The Square, Wimborne BH21 20 D4
The Sweep BH24 18 C4
The Topiary BH14 53 H1
The Triangle, Bournemouth BH2 4 C4
The Triangle, Poole BH16 34 D3
The Triangle*, Naish Est BH25 47 D7
The Ventura Centre BH16 34 F3
The Vineries BH21 21 G3
The Vinery BH25 48 D4
The Willows BH25 49 C7
The Woodrisings BH2 4 A2
Theobald Rd BH23 17 E3
Thetchers BH25 48 C2
Thetford Rd BH12 55 E1
Thistle CI BH23 45 F5
Thistlebarrow Rd BH7 41 G6
Thomas Lockyer CI BH31 7 C3
Thoresby Ct BH25 46 F4
Thorn Rd BH17 37 E2
Thornbury Rd BH6 59 G3
Thorncombe CI, Bournemouth BH9 41 E1
Thorncombe CI, Poole BH17 37 F3
Thorne CI BH31 7 B2
Thorne Way BH21 47 A6
Thornfield Dr BH23 47 A6
Thornham Rd BH25 48 E4
Thornley Rd BH10 32 A6
Thornton CI BH21 27 E5
Three Acre CI BH25 49 A6
Three Acre Rd BH25 49 A6
Three Cross Cotts BH21 8 A5
Three Lions CI BH21 20 D4
Throop CI BH8 42 A4
Throop Rd BH8 33 G6
Throopside Av BH9 33 F6
Thrush Rd BH12 38 B3
Thursby Rd BH23 44 B3
Thwaite Rd BH12 55 G1
Tidemill CI BH23 43 G5
Tiffany CI SO41 50 B1
Tilburg Rd BH23 60 A1
Tiller Gdns BH11 31 F5
Timothy CI BH10 31 H5
Tincleton Gdns BH9 40 D1
Todber CI BH11 38 D1
Tollard CI BH12 38 D5
Tollerford Rd BH17 37 F3
Tolpuddle Gdns BH9 33 E6
Tolstoi Rd BH14 53 H1
Tonge Rd BH11 31 G5
Top La BH24 18 C5
Torbay Rd BH14 54 B3
Totland Ct SO41 51 C3
Totmel Rd BH17 37 H2
Tourney Rd BH11 30 D5
Tower Ct BH2 4 B5
Tower Farm BH21 26 F3
Tower La BH21 21 F2
Tower Rd, Bournemouth BH1 57 G1
Tower Rd, Poole BH13 55 F5
Tower Rd West BH13 55 F5
Towers Way BH21 26 F3
Towngate Bri BH15
Towngate Shop Centre BH15 53 E4
Towngate Shopping Centre BH15 6 C3
Townsend CI BH11 31 G5
Townsville Rd BH9 40 D2
Tozer CI BH11 39 E3

Tracey Ct BH23 47 B7
Trafalgar Ct BH23 60 C2
Trafalgar Rd BH9 40 C5
Tree Hamlets BH16 34 E4
Treebys CI BH23 44 A4
Treeside BH23 45 G4
Trefoil Way BH23 45 F5
Tregonwell Rd BH2 4 C4
Trent Way BH22 24 D2
Trentham Av BH7 42 B6
Trentham CI BH7 42 B6
Tresillian CI BH23 47 C5
Tresillian Way BH23 47 C5
Tricketts La BH22 24 C2
Trigon Rd BH15 37 F6
Trinidad Cres BH12 38 B5
Trinidad Ho BH12 38 B4
Trinity BH1 5 F3
Trinity Rd BH1 5 F3
Troak CI BH23 44 B6
Troon Rd BH18 28 C5
Trotters La BH21 22 B2
Truman Rd BH11 31 G5
Trumpeters Ct BH21 20 D4
Truscott Av BH9 40 C5
Trystworthy BH2 4 B3
Tuckers La BH15 52 B5
Tucks CI BH23 64 B2
Tuckton CI BH6 58 D3
Tuckton Rd BH6 58 D4
Tudor Ct BH15 53 G1
Tudor Rd BH18 28 C6
Turbary CI BH12 38 D5
Turbary Ct BH16 34 E2
Turbary Park Av BH11 39 E1
Turbary Rd, Ferndown BH22 24 B2
Turbary Rd, Poole BH12 38 C5
Turbary Retail Pk BH11 38 D2
Turks La BH14 53 H6
Turlin Rd BH16 35 D6
Turnberry CI BH23 59 F2
Turners Farm Cres SO41 50 C3
Turnworth CI BH18 37 E1
Tweedale Rd BH9 41 E1
Twemlow Av BH14 53 G4
Twin Oaks CI BH18 36 C2
Twyford CI BH8 41 G2
Twyford Way BH17 38 A2
Twynham Av BH23 59 G1
Twynham Rd BH6 59 E4
Tynedale CI BH9 33 E6
Tyneham Av BH12 38 B5
Tyrrell Gdns BH8 42 A3
Tyrrells Ct BH23 64 C1
Tytherley Grn BH8 41 F2

Ubsdell CI BH25 48 B3
Uddens Dr BH21 12 C6
Uddens Trading Est BH21 22 D2
Ullswater Rd BH21 21 E6
Undercliff Dr BH1 5 E5
Undercliff Rd BH5 57 G4
Underwood CI BH17 36 D3
Uplands Av BH25 49 C7
Uplands CI BH22 14 C6
Uplands Gdns BH8 41 E3
Uplands Rd, Bournemouth BH8 41 E3
Uplands Rd, Ferndown BH22 14 C4
Uplyme CI BH17 37 H2
Upper Golf Links Rd BH18 28 D5
Upper Gordon Rd BH23 47 C6
Upper Hinton Rd BH1 5 E4
Upper Norwich Rd BH2 4 B4
Upper Rd BH12 38 B6
Upper Terrace Rd BH2 4 C4
Uppleby Rd BH12 54 B2
Upton By-Pass BH16,17 34 D2
Upton CI BH16 34 D2
Upton Ct BH16 34 E3
Upton Heath Est BH16 34 E3
Upton Pine Est BH18 36 B2
Upton Rd BH17 36 A5
Upton Way BH18 36 A1
Upwey Av BH15 52 A3

Vaggs La SO41 48 F1
Vale CI BH14 54 D2
Vale Mansions BH11 57 F3
Vale Rd, Bournemouth BH1 57 F3
Vale Rd, Poole BH14 54 D2

Valencia CI BH23 42 D2
Valette Rd BH9 40 D1
Valiant Way BH21 61 E1
Valley CI BH23 43 E3
Valley Rd BH8 41 H2
Valley Vw BH12 39 G5
Vallis CI BH15 6 D5
Vanguard Rd, Bournemouth BH8 41 H3
Vanguard Rd, Poole BH15 6 C3
Vantage Way BH12 38 A3
Vecta CI BH23 61 F1
Vectis Rd BH25 47 E7
Velvet Lawn Rd BH25 48 A3
Venator PI BH21 21 E2
Venning Av BH11 30 D5
Ventry CI BH13 55 E2
Ventura Pl BH16 34 E3
Verity Cres BH17 37 H4
Vernalls CI BH10 32 A5
Vernalls CI BH25 48 E2
Vernalls Gdns BH10 32 A5
Verne Rd BH31 7 D3
Verney CI BH11 39 F2
Verney Gdns BH11 39 F2
Verney Rd BH11 39 F1
Verno La BH23 45 G4
Verona Av BH6 58 D3
Verulam PI BH1 4 D3
Verulam Rd BH14 53 G3
Verwood Cres BH6 59 G3
Verwood Ind Est BH31 7 D2
Verwood Rd BH21 8 B4
Vetch CI BH23 45 F5
Vian Ct BH25 48 B4
Vicarage Gdns SO41 50 B3
Vicarage La SO41 50 B2
Vicarage Rd, Bournemouth BH9 40 B3
Vicarage Rd, Poole BH15 53 E1
Vicarage Rd, Verwood BH31 7 C2
Vicarage Way BH23 44 A3
Vickers CI BH8 42 B4
Vickery Way BH23 44 B6
Victoria Av BH9 40 B3
Victoria CI BH21 27 E6
Victoria Cres BH12 54 C1
Victoria Gdns, Ferndown BH22 24 A2
Victoria Gdns, Ringwood BH24 18 C5
Victoria Park Rd BH9 40 A3
Victoria PI, Bournemouth BH1 57 F1
Victoria Pl, Wimborne BH21 20 C3
Victoria Rd, Bournemouth BH1 57 E2
Victoria Rd, Christchurch BH23 60 C2
Victoria Rd, Ferndown BH22 24 A2
Victoria Rd, Lymington SO41 51 C3
Victoria Rd, Poole BH12 54 B2
Victoria Rd, Wimborne BH21 20 C3
Victory CI BH21 8 D6
Viewside CI BH21 27 E5
Viking CI BH6 59 F3
Viking Way, Bournemouth BH6 59 G4
Viking Way, Christchurch BH23 61 E3
Villette CI BH23 43 G5
Vince CI BH11 31 G5
Vincent CI BH25 48 B4
Vincent Rd BH25 48 B4
Vine CI BH7 42 A6
Vine Farm CI BH12 39 G4
Vine Farm Rd BH12 39 G4
Vine Hill BH21 20 A3
Vinegar Hill SO41 51 D3
Vineries CI BH21 21 G2
Vinneys CI BH23 44 A3
Violet Farm CI BH21 26 F2
Violet La BH25 48 C3
Virginia CI BH12 38 B6
Viscount CI BH11 30 C5
Viscount Dr BH23 61 E1
Viscount Walk BH11 30 B5
Vista Marina BH13 63 E3
Vixen Walk BH25 48 C2
Vulcan Way BH23 61 E1

Wagtail Dr BH25 48 A4
Wainsford Rd SO41 50 B5
Wakefield Av BH10 32 A6
Wakely Gdns BH11 31 F5
Wakely Rd BH11 31 F5
Walcheren Pl BH15 35 E6
Walcott Av BH23 42 D4
Walditch Gdns BH17 37 G2
Waldren CI BH15 53 F5
Walford CI BH21 20 D2
Walford Gdns BH21 20 D2
Walford Rd BH23 47 E5
Walford Way BH23 47 C6
Walking Field La BH15 6 D4
Walkwood Av BH7 42 B6
Wallace Rd BH18 36 C1
Wallis Rd BH10 39 G4
Walliscott Rd BH11 39 F3
Wallisdown Rd BH10,11,12 38 C2
Walnut CI BH25 48 B4
Walnut Tree Cotts BH23 33 E3
Walpole Rd BH1 57 G2
Walsford Rd BH4 55 H2
Walsingham Dene BH7 41 H5
Waltham Rd BH7 58 B1
Walton Rd, Bournemouth BH10 39 H3
Walton Rd, Poole BH15 37 H6
Wanstead CI BH24 19 E3
Warbler CI BH16 34 D2
Warburton Rd BH17 37 G4
Wareham CI BH7 58 B1
Wareham Rd BH21 27 C7
Warland Way BH21 28 A3
Warmwell CI, Bournemouth BH9 41 E1
Warmwell CI, Poole BH17 37 H3
Warnford Rd BH6,7 42 B6
Warren Av BH23 60 C3
Warren CI BH24 16 D2
Warren Dr BH24 16 D2
Warren Edge CI BH6 59 F5
Warren Edge Rd BH6 59 F4
Warren La BH24 16 D2
Warren Pk SO41 51 A1
Warren Rd, Bournemouth BH4 55 G4
Warren Rd, Poole BH14 54 C3
Warren Walk BH22 23 G1
Warwick Av BH25 48 C4
Warwick Rd, Bournemouth BH7 58 A2
Warwick Rd, Poole BH14 54 B4
Washington Av BH1 57 F1
Watcombe Rd BH6 58 D3
Water La BH6 42 D6
Water Tower Rd BH18 28 D6
Waterditch Rd BH23 44 C2
Waterford CI BH14 54 A5
Waterford Gdns BH23 47 B7
Waterford Pl BH23 47 C7
Waterford Rd, Christchurch BH23 47 C7
Waterford Rd, New Milton BH25 48 D4
Waterloo Ho BH17 36 D3
Waterloo Rd, Bournemouth BH9 40 C5
Waterloo Rd, Poole BH17 36 D5
Waterloo Way, Wimborne BH21 26 D4
Waterloo Way BH24 18 D5
Watermead BH23 59 G2
Watermill Rd BH23 43 G6
Waters Edge BH13 63 E2
Watership Dr BH24 19 F6
Waterside BH23 60 C3
Waterside BH24 18 D2
Watery La, Christchurch BH23 44 D5
Watery La, Poole BH16 34 A3
Watkin Rd BH5 57 H3
Watton CI BH8 42 A3
Wavell Av BH17 36 C4
Wavell Rd BH11 39 G1
Wavendon Av BH25 47 F7
Waverley Cres BH15 53 F1
Waverley Rd, Bournemouth BH1 57 E3
Waverley Rd, New Milton BH25 49 C5
Wayground Rd BH21 28 A1
Wayman Rd BH21 28 A4

Wayne Rd BH12 54 A1
Wayside CI SO41 51 D2
Wayside Rd, Bournemouth BH6 59 E4
Wayside Rd, Ringwood BH24 15 G5
Waytown CI BH17 37 E3
Weavers CI BH22 14 B5
Webbs CI BH24 9 G6
Webbs Way, Bournemouth BH11 39 E3
Webbs Way, Ringwood BH24 15 G1
Webster Rd BH9 40 D2
Wedgewood Gdns BH23 64 D1
Wedgwood Dr BH14 54 A5
Weldon Av BH11 30 D5
Well CI BH25 49 A5
Well La BH15 53 E2
Welland Rd BH21 21 E4
Wellesley Av BH23 45 F6
Wellington Av BH23 45 F6
Wellington Ct, Bournemouth BH2 4 A3
Wellington Ct, New Milton BH25 48 C3
Wellington Ho BH8 56 D2
Wellington Rd, Bournemouth BH8 5 G1
Wellington Rd, Poole BH14 54 B3
Wendover CI BH25 49 A6
Wendy Cres BH22 24 B5
Wenlock Ct*, Hunt Rd BH23 44 D5
Wentwood Gdns BH25 49 E5
Wentworth Av BH5 58 A4
Wentworth CI BH5 58 B4
Wentworth Dr, Broadstone BH18 28 C6
Wentworth Dr, Christchurch BH23 59 F2
Wescott Way BH11 38 D1
Wesley CI BH8 57 F1
Wesley Rd, Poole BH12 54 B2
Wesley Rd, Wimborne BH21 21 F3
Wessex Av BH25 49 B5
Wessex CI BH23 45 F6
Wessex Est BH24 19 E3
Wessex Gate Retail Pk BH15 36 C6
Wessex Rd, Poole BH14 54 A3
Wessex Rd, Ringwood BH24 19 E4
Wessex Trade Centre BH12 38 A5
Wessex Way BH1,2,4,8 4 A3
Wessx Way BH8 42 A5
West Av BH21 8 A4
West Borough BH21 20 D3
West Butts St BH15 6 B3
West CI, Bournemouth BH6 59 G3
West CI, Verwood BH31 7 A2
West Cliff Cotts BH2 4 B5
West Cliff Gdns BH2 4 B5
West Cliff Mews BH2 4 C6
West Cliff Prom BH2 4 C6
West Cliff Rd BH2,4 4 A5
West Hill PI BH2 4 B4
West Hill Rd BH2 4 B4
West Howe CI BH11 31 F6
West Howe Ind Est BH11 38 D2
West La SO41 50 B4
West Moors Rd, Ferndown BH22 24 A2
West Moors Rd, Three Legged Cross BH21 8 A4
West Overcliff Dr BH4 4 A6
West Overcliff Dr BH4 56 A5
West Quay Rd BH15 6 A5
West Rd, Bournemouth BH5 58 B3
West Rd, Christchurch BH23 64 B3
West Rd, Lymington SO41 51 B2
West Row Row BH21 20 D4
West St, Poole BH15 6 A5
West St, Ringwood BH24 18 B5
West St, Wimborne BH21 20 D4
West Station Ter BH2 4 A3

West Undercliff Prom BH2	4 B6	White Cl BH15	38 A6	Wills Rd BH12	55 E2	Wishart Gdns BH9	33 E6	Woolslope Gdns BH22	14 B5
West View Rd, Christchurch BH23	60 B2	White Farm Cl BH10	40 A4	Willwood Cl BH17	37 F2	Wistaria Ho BH10	32 C6	Woolslope Rd BH22	14 B5
West View Rd, Poole BH15	6 B1	White Horse Dr BH15	53 F3	Wilmur Cres BH15	53 F1	Wisteria Dr BH31	7 F4	Woolven Cl BH14	53 H1
West Way, Bournemouth BH9	40 D2	White Horses BH15	49 A8	Wilson Rd, Bournemouth BH1	57 G1	Witchampton Rd BH18	36 B2	Wootton Gdns BH1	5 F3
West Way, Broadstone BH18	36 A2	White Knights BH25	49 B8	Wilson Rd, Poole BH14	54 B2	Withermoor Rd BH9	40 B4	Wootton Mount BH1	5 F3
West Way Cl BH9	41 E3	White Lion Courtyard BH24	18 B5	Wilton Cl BH23	42 D5	Withingham Rd BH13	55 E3	Worbarrow Gdns BH12	38 A6
Westbeams Rd SO41	64 C5	Whitebeam Way BH31	7 E3	Wilton Gdns BH25	48 A4	Witney Rd BH17	37 E4	Wordsworth Av BH8	41 G3
Westbourne Cl BH4	55 H3	Whitecliff Cres BH14	53 H5	Wilton Rd BH7	58 A3	Woking Rd BH14	54 B2	Worgret Rd BH15	37 E6
Westbourne Park Rd BH4	55 G5	Whitecliff Rd BH14	53 G4	Wiltshire Gdns BH23	64 A2	Wolfe Cl BH23	44 B6	Worley Way BH22	24 B5
Westbrook Cl BH10	40 A3	Whitecross Cl BH17	37 F2	Wiltshire Rd BH23	64 A2	Wollaston Rd BH6	59 F5	Worrell Dr BH17	38 B5
Westbury Cl, Bransgore BH23	64 B3	Whitefield Rd, New Milton BH25	48 B4	Wilverley Av BH8	41 H3	Wollaton Cres BH22	23 H6	Worthington Cres BH14	54 A4
Westbury Cl, New Milton BH25	49 C6	Whitefield Rd, Poole BH14	53 H4	Wilverley Rd BH23	44 D6	Wollaton Rd BH22	23 H6	Worthy Rd BH25	48 B4
Westbury Cl, Sway BH23	45 G4	Whitehall BH23	59 H2	Wimborne By-Pass BH21	20 B6	Wollstonecraft Rd BH5	57 H3	Wortley Rd BH23	47 B7
Westbury Ct BH14	54 A3	Whitehart Flds BH24	19 E3	Wimborne Rd, Bournemouth BH2	4 D2	Wolseley Rd BH12	54 C1	Wraxall Cl BH17	37 E3
Westbury Rd BH24	19 E5	Whitehayes Cl BH23	44 A4	Wimborne Rd, Bournemouth BH10,11	31 E5	Wolsey Way SO41	51 E3	Wren Cl, Christchurch BH23	61 E3
Westby Rd BH5	57 H3	Whitehayes Rd BH23	44 A4	Wimborne Rd, Bournemouth BH3,9	40 B6	Wolterton Rd BH12	55 F1	Wren Cl, New Milton BH25	49 A5
Westcroft Pk BH18	37 E1	Whitehouse Rd BH21	21 E6	Wimborne Rd, Colehill BH21	21 F2	Wolverton Rd BH7	57 H1	Wren Cl, Ringwood BH24	19 E6
Westdown Rd BH11	31 F5	Whitelegg Way BH10	32 B5	Wimborne Rd, Corfe Mullen BH21	26 F2	Wood La, Bournemouth BH11	30 D4	Wren Cres BH12	55 F1
Westerham BH13	55 G3	Whiteways BH21	21 F2	Wimborne Rd, Knobcrook BH21	20 D2	Wood La, Lymington SO41	51 D3	Wroxham Rd BH12	55 E2
Westerham Rd BH4	55 G3	Whitfield Pk BH24	16 B2	Wimborne Rd, Poole BH15	6 C2	Wood Lawn Cl BH25	49 A6	Wyatts Cl BH21	27 E5
Western Av, Bournemouth BH10	32 A6	Whitingham Ct BH5	58 B2	Wimborne Rd, Wimborne Minster BH21	20 A6	Wood Vw BH21	11 H6	Wyatts Rd BH21	26 E4
Western Av, New Milton BH25	47 E6	Whitley Way BH25	48 C2	Wimborne Rd East BH22	23 F2	Woodacre Gdns BH22	24 A4	Wychwood Cl BH2	4 C1
Western Av, Poole BH13	54 D4	Whitsbury Cl BH8	41 F3	Wimborne Rd West BH21	22 A4	Woodbury BH1	5 F5	Wychwood Dr BH2	4 D1
Western Cl BH10	31 H6	Whittle Rd BH21	23 E1	Winchester Pl BH15	6 C3	Woodbury Av BH8	41 H3	Wychwood Grange BH2	4 D1
Western Rd BH13	55 E6	Whittles Way BH15	6 A3	Winchester Rd BH25	48 D2	Woodbury Ct BH23	43 E2	Wycliffe Rd BH9	40 B5
Westfield Cl BH21	20 D3	Wick 1 Ind Est BH25	48 A4	Wincombe Cl BH22	24 A5	Woodcock La SO41	50 C2	Wyelands Av BH21	22 C3
Westfield Gdns BH23	45 E5	Wick 2 Ind Est BH25	47 F5	Wincombe Dr BH22	24 A5	Woodcocks Cres BH7	42 A6	Wykeham Cl BH17	37 F5
Westfield Rd BH6	59 E3	Wick Cl BH25	47 F5	Windermere Rd BH3	40 D6	Woodcote Dr BH16	34 D3	Wyncombe Rd BH5	58 B2
Westgate Pk BH4	55 G3	Wick Dr BH25	49 A5	Windgreen BH21	26 F3	Woodend BH1		Wyndham Cl BH23	47 D5
Westham BH17	37 F1	Wick La, Christchurch BH23	59 G2	Windham Mews BH1	57 G1	Woodend Rd, Bournemouth BH9	40 B5	Wyndham Rd, Christchurch BH23	47 D5
Westheath Rd BH18	28 C6	Wick La, Southbourne BH6,23	59 F3	Windham Rd BH1	57 E2	Woodend Rd, Ringwood BH24	19 G6	Wyndham Rd, Poole BH14	54 A3
Westland Dr BH13	63 F1	Wick Point Mews BH23	59 G2	Windmill Cl, Lymington SO41	51 D3	Woodfield Gdns BH23	45 G4	Wynford Rd, Bournemouth BH9	40 D1
Westlands BH22	64 B2	Wicket Rd BH10	31 H5	Windmill Cl, Ringwood BH24	16 D3	Woodfield Rd BH11	31 F6	Wynford Rd, Poole BH14	54 B3
Westminster Ct BH25	49 A8	Wickfield Av BH23	59 G2	Windmill La BH24	16 D3	Woodford Cl BH24	19 E5	Wynne Cl BH18	28 B6
Westminster Rd, Lymington SO41	51 B3	Wickfield Cl BH23	59 G2	Windsor Cl, Lymington SO41	50 A1	Woodford Rd BH1	57 E3	Wynter Cl BH7	41 H5
Westminster Rd, Poole BH13	55 F5	Wickham Ct BH22	24 B2	Windsor Cl, Ringwood BH24	15 H2	Woodgreen Dr BH11	30 C6	Wyvern Cl BH12	38 C5
Westminster Rd East BH13	55 G6	Wickham Dr BH21	27 F6	Windsor Ct, Christchurch BH23	47 B7	Woodhayes Av BH23	45 H4	
Westmoreland Ct SO41	50 A2	Wickham Rd BH7	58 A3	Windsor Ct, Poole BH14	54 B3	Woodlake Cl BH17	37 E3	Yarmouth Cl BH12	55 F2
Weston Dr BH1	5 H3	Wicklea Rd BH6	59 H3	Windsor Rd, Bournemouth BH5	57 G3	Woodland Av BH5	58 A4	Yarmouth Rd BH12	55 E1
Weston Rd BH21	21 H1	Wickmeads Rd BH6	59 F3	Windsor Rd, Christchurch BH23	43 E6	Woodland Cl BH31	7 B1	Yarrells Dr BH16	34 D3
Westons La BH15	6 B4	Widden Cl SO41	64 C5	Windsor Rd, Poole BH14	54 A4	Woodland Walk, Bournemouth BH5	58 A3	Yarrells La BH16	34 E4
Westover La BH24	16 D1	Widdicombe Av BH14	54 D5	Winfrith Cres BH14	38 D5	Woodland Walk, Ferndown BH22	24 B1	Yarrow Cl BH23	45 E5
Westover Rd, Bournemouth BH1	5 E4	Widget Cl BH11	39 G2	Wingfield Av, Christchurch BH23	36 A5	Woodland Way, Christchurch BH23	45 H6	Yarrow Rd BH12	37 H5
Westover Rd, Lymington SO41	51 D3	Widworthy Dr BH18	28 B5	Wingfield Av, Poole BH15	53 F1	Woodland Way, Lymington SO41	51 C3	Yeatminster Rd BH17	37 G3
Westwood Av BH22	23 H3	Wight Walk BH22	24 A6	Wingfield Ct BH1	57 E4	Woodlands BH13	55 F3	Yelverton Rd BH1	4 D3
Westwoods Pk BH25	46 F1	Wilderton Rd BH13	55 E4	Winifred Rd BH15	53 F2	Woodlands Av BH15	52 A3	Yeomans Ind Est BH8	41 G2
Wetherby Cl BH18	36 C3	Wilderton Rd West BH13	55 E3	Winkton Cl BH23	44 A3	Woodlands Cl BH23	64 B2	Yeomans Ind Pk BH8	41 H2
Weymans Av BH10	31 H4	Wildfell Cl BH23	43 G5	Winkton Ho BH23	43 F6	Woodlands Cres BH15	52 A4	Yeomans Rd BH8	41 G3
Weymans Dr BH10	31 H4	Wildown Gdns BH6	59 F4	Winnards Cl BH22	24 B6	Woodlands Rd BH25	49 A8	Yeomans Way BH8	41 G2
Weymouth Rd BH14	54 B2	Wildown Rd BH6	59 F5	Winniford Cl BH23	45 G4	Woodlands Way, New Milton BH25	48 C1	Yeovilton Cl SO41	50 B5
Wharf Cl BH12	38 D6	Wilfred Rd BH5	57 H3	Winsley Av BH6	58 C4	Woodlands Way, Ringwood BH24	15 H2	Yerville Gdns SO41	50 A2
Wharfdale Rd, Bournemouth BH4	4 A3	Wilkins Way BH15	6 A4	Winspit Cl BH15	52 A4	Woodleaze Cl BH18	28 D4	Yew La BH25	48 D3
Wharfdale Rd, Poole BH14	38 D6	Wilkinson Dr BH8	42 B4	Winston Av BH12	39 E6	Woodlinken Cl BH31	7 E4	Yew Tree Cl BH21	21 E4
Wharncliffe Ct BH23	47 A8	Willett Rd BH21	20 B6	Winston Cl BH25	49 B6	Woodlinken Dr BH31	7 E4	York Av BH25	48 C4
Wharncliffe Gdns BH23	47 B7	William Cl BH23	47 C5	Winston Ct*, Stour Rd BH23	59 G1	Woodlinken Way BH31	7 E4	York Cl, Broadstone BH18	36 C2
Wharncliffe Rd, Bournemouth BH5	57 G3	William Rd BH7	41 H6	Winston Gdns BH12	39 F6	Woodpecker Cl BH31	7 C3	York Cl, Christchurch BH23	43 F6
Wharncliffe Rd, Christchurch BH23	47 A7	William St BH23	47 C7	Winston Pk BH12	39 E6	Woodpecker Dr BH17	36 A5	York Pl, Bournemouth BH7	58 A2
Whatleigh Cl BH15	6 C4	Williams Ind Pk BH25	47 F5	Winston Rd BH9	40 D2	Woodruff Cl BH23	45 F5	York Pl, New Milton BH25	48 C4
Wheaton Grange BH4	4 A2	Willis Cl BH21	27 F6	Winston Way BH24	18 D4	Woods Edge BH18	36 C2	York Rd, Bournemouth BH1	5 H3
Wheaton Rd BH7	58 A2	Willis Way BH15	36 D6	Winterbourne Cl BH15	53 F2	Woods View Rd BH9	40 A4	York Rd, Broadstone BH18	36 B3
Wheelers La BH11	30 C5	Willow Cl, Bournemouth BH4	55 G2	Winterbourne Rd BH15	53 F2	Woodside Cl BH22	24 A2	Youngs Rd BH11	31 F6
Whimbrel Ct BH23	60 D2	Willow Cl, Poole BH16	34 F4	Winterhayes Cl BH17	37 F2	Woodside Rd, Bournemouth BH5	58 B3	
Whincroft Cl BH22	24 B2	Willow Cl, Ringwood BH24	15 F2	Winton Way BH10	40 A3	Woodside Rd, Ferndown BH22	24 A2	Zamek Cl BH11	31 F6
Whincroft Dr BH22	24 A2	Willow Ct BH7	58 C1	Winton Way, New Milton BH25	48 D4	Woodside Rd, Poole BH14	54 B3	Zetland Ct BH4	55 G5
Whitby Av BH18	36 B3	Willow Dr, Christchurch BH23	59 F2	Wisbech Way SO41	50 B3	Woodside Rd, West Moors BH22	14 A2	Zinnia Cl BH10	40 A3
Whitby Cl BH23	42 D2	Willow Dr, Ringwood BH24	18 D6			Woodstock Cl*, Woodstock Rd BH4	54 A5	
Whitby Cres BH18	36 B3	Willow Dr, Wimborne BH21	22 B3			Woodstock La BH24	18 C5	
Whitby Ct BH23	51 C3	Willow Mead BH8	33 F6			Woodstock Rd, Christchurch BH23	44 A3	
Whitby Rd SO41	51 B3	Willow Pk BH14	53 H3			Woodstock Rd, Poole BH14	54 A5	
Whitchurch Av BH18	37 E1	Willow Pl BH23	59 H1			Woodvale Gdns BH25	48 D3	
White Barn Cres SO41	50 C2	Willow Tree Rise BH11	39 G2			Wool Rd BH14	38 A4	
		Willow Walk BH25	49 C8			Woolmer La BH24	18 C1	
		Willow Way, Christchurch BH23	59 F2			Woolsbridge Ind Pk BH21	8 D6	
		Willow Way, Ferndown BH22	23 H1			Woolsbridge Rd BH24	15 H1	
		Willowdene Cl BH25	48 D4			Woolslope Cl BH22	14 B6	

Edition 105-15 08.04